# Contents

# ACKNOWLEDGEMENTS

I should like to thank Hilla Patell and Muriel Dwyer for their support, encouragement and inspiration over the last 20 years; Renilde Montessori for her unceasing energy as the General Secretary for AMI as she travels the world inspiring those who believe that Montessori education is an education for life, and for taking time out from a busy schedule to advise me on the biography; and Rosemary Sassoon, whose understanding of children's handwriting is outstanding and whose passion is infectious! Jesse Scott, James Irwin and Eve Lawrence kindly worked their way through the early versions of the book and thanks, too, to Hilary White for her shared interest and expertise. I am very grateful to my editor Isabel Moore for her enthusiasm and understanding and to the photographer Ron Sutherland whose beautiful photographs are proof of his ability to work well with children. Isabel, Ron and I had an intense but hugely enjoyable time working with the children of the Maria Montessori Children's House. Thanks must also go to the children, parents, students and staff of the Maria Montessori Training Organisation who collaborated so enthusiastically, and to Scilla Towns for help in compiling the book lists. Finally, I must thank my family and friends for all the support they so willingly gave as I wrote this book.

## Publisher's note

# Montessori Read and Write

## A Parents' Guide to Literacy for Children

Lynne Lawrence

EBURY PRESS

LONDON

DEDICATION
*To Steve, Tom and Jamie*

First published in 1998

1 3 5 7 9 10 8 6 4 2

Text © Lynne Lawrence 1998
Photographs © Ebury Press or Ron Sutherland 1998

First published in the United Kingdom in 1998 by
Ebury Press
Random House, 20 Vauxhall Bridge Road, London
SW1V 2SA

Random House Australia (Pty) Limited
20 Alfred Street, Milsons Point, Sydney,
New South Wales 2061, Australia

Random House New Zealand Limited
18 Poland Road, Glenfield, Auckland 10, New Zealand

Random House South Africa (Pty) Limited
Endulini, 5a Jubilee Road, Parktown 2193, South Africa

Random House UK Limited Reg. No. 954009

Papers used by Ebury Press are natural, recyclable
products made from wood grown in sustainable forests.

A CIP catalogue record for this book is available from
the British Library.

ISBN 0 09 186351 1

Project editor Isabel Moore
Designed by Jerry Goldie
Photography by Ron Sutherland

Printed and bound in Italy by
New Interlitho Italia S.p.a.

# Introduction

Over the last 20 years I have watched countless children master the arts of reading and writing in an effortless and enjoyable way. There are no big secrets to this – it is not a question of money and it is not difficult. What I am certain of, is that the process is easy and natural under the age of six. After six it is, at best, an uphill struggle.

This book is not written for my peers or for the students I teach; nor is it written to persuade sceptics of the value of the Montessori approach, or to challenge any prevailing notions of what constitutes the best method of teaching reading and writing. It is simply written for those parents who want to offer practical help to their children along the path to literacy.

Many parents get locked out of the process of helping their child to read and write because our cultural attitude tells them that it is difficult and that it is something for teachers to do. This really should not be so. The preparation for reading and writing begins long before formal school and parents are the first and best teachers.

I am also convinced that literacy is the only way for children to burst out of the cultural and social bindings which constrain their lives, to lift their sights and extend their horizons, and ultimately to play their part in advancing our society.

The ability to read and write is not, in itself, a sufficient ambition. What is of supreme importance is bringing about, in a child, a desire to read and write: this is the Holy Grail.

This book is not for just dipping into as the whim takes you. It charts a developmental process with activities that fit with the maturational process in a young mind. It is like building a house on solid foundations, each brick upon another and finally a roof. If you build a precarious tower on sand, it may look good for a while, but it will fall down.

The foundations for literacy are love and encouragement. The basement is constructed from the joy of being read to, knowledge of the world, a language-rich environment, development of the senses and control of the body. The ground floor rooms are made from an awareness of the sounds in language. The upper floor is created from the ability to attach symbols to sounds and the attic is made from the skill of using those symbols to express your own thoughts. The roof is reading and writing. In such a house a child's mind can reside for a rewarding lifetime and no hurricane can blow it down.

In each chapter of this book you will find important activities which are the building blocks of literacy; they reflect the kinds of activities, but are not necessarily the same as those, that go on in a Montessori school. In addition, there are lots of games that are ideally suited for parents to engage in with their children at home.

Read each chapter before you embark on helping your child towards reading and writing, as it will give you a feel for the overall approach, which requires you to follow a number of parallel paths. As a rough guide you will find that Chapters 1 and 2 relate to the general Montessori approach; Chapter 3 provides activities that underpin reading and writing; Chapter 4 contains three essential activities that are the gateway to reading and writing; Chapters 5 and 6 must be read in parallel with each other as they develop your child's ability to read and write; Chapters 7 and 8 must also be read in parallel as they develop more sophisticated skills in reading and writing; and Chapter 9 contains advice on how to make some of the activities referred to in this book and provides you with templates to use.

Please remember as you go that, in young children of three or four, reading does not precede writing – these abilities progress hand in hand, with writing initially slightly ahead leading the way. Children who have learned in a Montessori environment starting at about two and a half years old will, quite naturally, write before they read.

I have written this book as an aid for parents to use at home, and although it is complete in its own right it will also supplement any work being done in school. While parents are always the main educators of a young child, the role of the teacher is also important. A Montessori environment for a young child is a very appropriate solution to the pressures of modern life where parents seldom have the choice of being at home full-time. However, Montessori is more than just a kind of school, it is an attitude, an approach, and I hope that in reading this book you may come to understand a little about this approach and will feel inclined to follow it with your child.

Any shortcomings that you encounter in this book will be mine; they do not reflect on the Montessori approach.

If, as a result of reading this book, one parent helps one child to learn to love reading and writing then, for me, writing it will have been worthwhile.

Lynne Lawrence
*March 1998*

# About Maria Montessori

Maria Montessori was born in 1870 in the town of Chiarvalle, Italy. Her father, Alessandro, made a career in the civil service and her mother, Renilde Stoppani, was well educated and forward looking. Their house was apparently full of books for Renilde loved reading, a passion which she passed on to her daughter.

The Montessori family moved to Rome in 1875 and the following year the young Maria enrolled in the public school on the Via di San Nicolo da Tolentino. As her education progressed, she began to break through the barriers which constrained women's careers and from 1886 to 1890 she continued her studies at the Regio Istituto Tecnico Leonardo da Vinci – initially with the intention of becoming an engineer, unheard of for a woman. At some moment and for reasons she herself was unable to explain, she changed her mind about engineering as a career and decided to become a doctor of medicine.

At that time it was unthinkable that a woman should enter medical school. However, it seems that Pope Leo XIII interceded on her behalf and in 1890 she enrolled at the University of Rome, initially studying physics, mathematics and the natural sciences; in 1892 she passed her exams, receiving the Diploma di Licenza, her passport to the Faculty of Medicine.

At medical school her male colleagues were hostile to her presence and no doubt somewhat intimidated. For the sake of propriety, Maria found herself excluded from anatomy and dissecting classes – it was considered unseemly for a woman to look on a naked body in the company of her male colleagues – and so she undertook her dissection work on her own after hours.

Montessori's biographers relate the story of a seminal moment in her studies when, after an isolated evening in the dissecting room, she departed with the intention of abandoning her medical studies. On her way home she was confronted by a beggar woman with a two year-old child who was playing with a piece of coloured paper. She was deeply affected by the expression of happiness on the child's face and by its total absorption in the activity with the piece of paper, and later related that she was moved by emotions she could not herself explain to turn around and return directly to the dissecting room. Perhaps in the activity of this poverty-stricken child she had found her vocation.

In 1896 Maria Montessori graduated from the University of Rome with top honours as the first woman doctor in Italy. She was immediately employed in the San Giovanni Hospital attached to the University. Later that year she was asked to represent Italy at an International Congress for Women's Rights and in her speech to the Congress she developed a thesis for social reform, arguing that women should be entitled to equal wages with men.

In November 1896 Montessori added the appointment as surgical assistant at Santo Spirito Hospital in Rome to her portfolio of tasks. Much of her work there was with the poor, and particularly with the children of the poor. As a doctor she was noted for the way in which she 'tended' her patients, making sure they were warm and properly fed as well as diagnosing and treating their illnesses. In 1897 she volunteered to join a research programme at the psychiatric clinic of the University of Rome and it was here that she worked alongside Giusseppe Montesano with whom a romance was to develop.

As part of her work for the clinic she would visit Rome's asylums for the insane, seeking subjects for treatment at the clinic. She relates how, on one such visit when she saw a group of children in a bare unfurnished room, she realized that their environment deprived them of the sensorial stimulation for which they naturally craved, thereby contributing to their condition. She began to read all she could on the subject of mentally retarded children and in particular she studied the groundbreaking work of two early 19th century Frenchmen, Jean-Marc-Gaspard Itard and Edouard Seguin; she was so keen to understand their work properly that she translated it herself from French into Italian.

During the 1897-98 university terms she sought to expand her knowledge of education by attending courses in pedagogy and studied the work of Rousseau, Pestalozzi and Froebel. Froebel had in 1837 established a school for very young children – a radical innovation, which he called Kleinkinderbeschaefti-gungsanstalt, an appropriate but rather unwieldy title that has given way to the modern word Kindergarten. Froebel, convinced of the value of play in early learning, developed a series of toys or apparatus which he called 'gifts' and these anticipated the development of Montessori's materials.

In 1897 Montessori was asked to address the National Medical Congress in Turin, where she advocated the controversial theory that the lack of adequate care for retarded and disturbed children was a cause of their delinquency. She expanded on this in 1898 and in September of that year addressed the National Pedagogical Congress in Turin, presenting a vision of social progress and political economy rooted in commonly supported educational measures. The notion of social reform through education was an idea that was to develop and mature in Montessori's thinking throughout her life.

By the end of 1898 a committee had been formed to generate funds for a national medical-pedagogical institution, the National League for the Education of Retarded Children. As a representative of the League, Montessori embarked upon a lecture tour in 1899 which gave her the opportunity of synthesizing her arguments for the emancipation of women, the alleviation of poverty, the education of very young children and the foundation of a peaceful and prosperous civilization. Were she alive today promoting such ideas she would be considered ahead of her time, so it is worth reflecting for a moment that she was a young woman of twenty-seven speaking out a century ago.

Montessori's involvement with the National League for the Education of Retarded Children led to her appointment as co-director with Giusseppe Montesano of a new institution called the Orthophrenic School. This school took children with a broad spectrum of different disorders and disabilities and by July 1900 these children were showing such progress that official visits were made from various important institutions. Montessori spent two years working at the Orthophrenic School. She brought a scientific analytical attitude to her work, teaching and

ABOVE **Maria Montessori.**

observing by day and writing up notes by night. She acknowledged this period as being the time she truly came to understand pedagogy, and it was here that she first developed ideas for her educational materials, going far beyond the ideas of Seguin, Itard and Froebel.

The relationship with Giusseppe Montesano had developed into a love affair and in 1898

Maria gave birth to a child, a boy named Mario, who was given into the care of a family who lived in the countryside near Rome. Maria visited the child often but it was not until he was older that Mario came to know that Maria was his mother. Certainly a strong bond was maintained and in later years he collaborated and travelled with his mother, continuing her work after her death.

In 1901 Maria left the Orthophrenic School and immersed herself in her own studies into educational philosophy and anthropology;

subsequently, in 1904, she took up a post in the Pedagogic School of the University of Rome which she held until 1908.

Rome during this period was growing very rapidly and in the fever of speculative development some construction companies and landowners were falling into bankruptcy, leaving unfinished building projects which quickly attracted squatters. One such development stood in the San Lorenzo district between the old Roman wall and the cemetery. The building project was rescued by a group of wealthy bankers, the Beni Stabili group, who undertook a basic restoration creating a tenement block containing individual apartments, which were soon occupied by impoverished working families. With parents out at work all day the younger children wreaked havoc on the newly completed building and Beni Stabili sought help from Dr. Montessori to provide ways of occupying the children so that they would not damage the premises.

Montessori grasped the opportunity of working with normal children and, bringing some of the educational materials she had developed at the Orthophrenic School, she established her first Casa dei Bambini or 'Children's House'. Within three months a second Casa was opened. There was no expectation that she would achieve anything with these children, which gave her the opportunity to experiment. She put many things into the children's environment but kept only those that engaged them. What Montessori came to realize was that children who were placed in an environment where activities were designed to support their natural development had the power to educate themselves. She was to refer to this later as auto-education.

In 1914 she wrote,
*'I did not invent a method of Education, I simply gave some little children a chance to live'.*

It is a testament to her insight that contemporary discoveries about the way children grow, develop and learn consistently reinforce her conclusions.

The children in the Casa made extraordinary progress and soon five-year-olds were writing and reading. News of Montessori's new approach spread rapidly and visitors arrived to see for themselves how she was achieving such results. In the summer of 1909 she gave the first training course in her approach to early education to about one hundred students. Her notes from this period developed into The Montessori Method, which was subsequently published in the United States in 1912 and has become one of the most influential books ever written in the field of education.

On 20 December 1912 her mother died at the age of seventy-two. Maria was deeply affected by this event and in the year following her mother's death she brought her son Mario to Rome to be with her.

A period of great expansion in the Montessori approach now followed. Montessori societies, training programmes and schools sprang to life all over the world, and a period of travel with public speaking and lecturing occupied Montessori, much of it in America, but also in the United Kingdom and Holland. Thomas Edison and Alexander Graham Bell had invited her to America where a burgeoning Montessori movement was underway; Bell himself was the president of the American Montessori Society and Margaret Wilson, daughter of the then President of the United States, was its secretary. Much of the expansion, however, was ill-founded and distorted by the events of the First World War. It must have been very difficult for Maria, who had no independent income, to remain in touch with the broad spectrum of development which was going on in her name in so many parts of the world and she developed a growing concern about her legacy that was to culminate in the establishment of the Association Montessori Internationale (AMI) in 1929 in Denmark. Today AMI monitors the standards of 45 full-time training schools around the world for teachers of children from 0-3, 3-6 and 6-12.

On returning from America in 1917, and after Mario's marriage to his first wife Helen Christie, she based herself in Barcelona, Spain where a Seminari Laboratori di Pedagogia had been created for her. Her son and his new wife joined her and her four grandchildren were born there: two boys, Mario Jr. and Rolando, and two girls, Marilena and Renilde. Renilde, her youngest grandchild, is today the General Secretary of AMI.

Maria nursed an ambition to create a permanent centre for research and development into her approach to early years education, but any possibility of this happening in her lifetime in Spain was thwarted by the rise of fascism in Europe. By 1933 all Montessori schools in Germany had been closed and an effigy of her was burned above a bonfire of her books in Berlin; the Third Montessori Congress, scheduled for Berlin in 1934, was cancelled. In the same year, after Montessori refused to co-operate with Mussolini's plans to incorporate Italian Montessori schools into the fascist youth movement, he closed them all down. The outbreak of civil war in Spain forced the family to abandon their home in Barcelona and they sailed to England in the summer of 1936. From England the refugees travelled to Holland to stay in the family home of Ada Pierson the daughter of a Dutch banker. Mario, by now estranged from his first wife, was later to marry Ada.

Plans were made to create a model school and research centre at Laren in Holland, and with Amsterdam now the headquarters of AMI

the future for the Montessoris looked promising. In 1939 Mario and Maria embarked on a journey to India to give a three-month training course in Madras followed by a lecture tour; they were not to return for nearly seven years. With the outbreak of war, as Italian citizens, Mario was interned and Maria put under house arrest. She spent the summer in Kodaikanal and this experience guided her thinking towards the nature of the relationship between all living things, a theme she was to develop until the end of her life and which became known as cosmic education, an approach for children between six and 12. Montessori was well looked after in India where she met Gandhi, Nehru and Tagore. Her 70th birthday request to the Indian government – that Mario should be released and restored to her – was granted, and together they gave courses to which hundreds of students came.

In 1946 they returned to Holland and to the grandchildren who had spent the war years in the care of Ada Pierson. In 1947 Montessori, now 76, addressed UNESCO on the theme 'Education and Peace'. In 1949 she received the first of three nominations for the Nobel Peace Prize and at the UNESCO Conference in Florence in 1950, the Director General Jaime Torres Bodet proclaimed her as the symbol for education and world peace.

Her last public engagement was in London in 1951 when she attended the Ninth International Montessori Congress. On 6 May 1952, in the house of the Pierson family in Holland, she died in the company of her beloved son Mario to whom she bequeathed the legacy of her work.

That work continues in all parts of the world and with children from all cultures and backgrounds and it is as relevant today as it ever was.

# What you should know about your child

Language is one of the most fascinating of human attributes. We watch it develop in young children but as yet understand very little about the process. We do now know that voices, particularly those of the mother and father, are points of reference for a newborn child. songs sung to a fetus in the womb will have a calming effect on a distraught newborn baby as she recognizes something that is familiar. After birth, the attraction a child has towards language, even when she literally cannot understand a word, is amazing.

As a parent you are the first and most important teacher of your child. The more in tune you are with the way she develops, therefore, the more successful you will be in providing what she needs. Language development in all children follows specific and observable patterns and once you understand what is happening you will feel confident about the help that you can offer your own child.

To help her to write and read well, you will need to begin to develop her ability to communicate with others about the things that she knows. It will be essential for her to have a good vocabulary, to be able to express herself confidently and to have heard a variety of sources of rich and interesting language. Research now shows that children with these good verbal skills find reading and writing easier.

If you wish your child to become a good 'reader' and 'writer' you will need to prepare the ground well in advance of these abilities developing, and you will need to spend time building up all the skills that are required for these two complex processes.

Don't be tempted to rush her. Your aim is to help her develop a love of reading and writing so that throughout her life she will choose to read and choose to write. If children develop a love of books and of reading, all the world's knowledge becomes available to them, all the stories, myths and legends, in fact and fiction. Each time they open a book they will become a time-traveller. For a moment, real time is suspended as they become engaged in the story. A book can take them to explore worlds known and unknown, can help them travel forwards and backwards in time. Children who become good readers will have the power to pursue their own interests beyond the limited information available from the adults around them, and children who become good writers will have ways of expressing their thoughts and feelings in more tangible and lasting forms.

There are many things that need to be done before your child can read or write and it is helpful if you do not have in mind a definite age for her to have mastered these skills.

Preparing your child to read and write means that you must first start to prepare for

RIGHT **If you can help your child develop a love of reading then not only will she be able to read but she will also choose to do so throughout her life.**

reading and writing 'readiness', and to do this you must have some knowledge of the basic Montessori principles that apply to child development in this area.

In the first six years of life all children:

◆ Have an absorbent mind.
◆ Have moments of acute sensitivity towards their environment, which are called 'sensitive periods'.
◆ Have strong urges to communicate, to be independent and to explore.
◆ Learn primarily through their senses and through movement.

## The absorbent mind

A child in the first six years of her life has a mind that functions very differently from an adult mind: it appears to absorb vast amounts of information without any effort on the part of the child. How does a child in just three years manage to create all the basic elements of language?

At birth she cannot speak any language, yet by three she has formed the basis of her language and by six has command of a wide vocabulary. Of course language will still develop after six but not in the same way. We also know that provided a child has an opportunity to hear language in this period, she will learn not just one language but as many as she is exposed to. In many parts of the world children of six are fluent in as many as three different languages: children in Kenya, for example, may come to a Montessori school at the age of three knowing a tribal language such as Kikuyu, their African language Swahili and English. Could you as an adult, in three short years, do as much? Not only do the Kenyan children learn the vocabulary of each language, they can also produce perfect sounds. No matter how long you took as an adult to learn a language you would never quite perfect the sounds in the way that a child can.

For the first three years of life a child is able simply to take in information from her surrounding environment without discrimination and without effort, creating and building all the basic building blocks of her personality and forming her mind. From the age of three on, she is still able to take in information but brings to this an element of choice and selectivity, and therefore makes a more conscious exploration of the world around her.

Imagine that a child's mind is like a sponge: if you place a sponge in water it will soak up the water, whether is it clean or dirty. A child's mind is like this – it will absorb, without effort, whatever it finds in the environment. A sponge, once placed in water, is very different from when it was dry – you could say that it has transformed itself; it is different underwater, it is soft and pliable. A child's mind is also transformed by what it takes in from the environment. The sponge, however, can only absorb so much water; the child's mind is not like this – it can absorb huge quantities of information simply by living.

Looking at a newborn baby you will notice that from the earliest days of life her attention is focused on the mouth of the person speaking to her. She appears to be drinking in the whole person while listening and looking intently at the mouth that speaks. We know that talking to a baby a lot significantly speeds up the process of learning new words.

The mind only functions like this in the first six years of life, and not only will a child acquire such obvious human characteristics as language, but also knowledge about the world and how it works and knowledge about values and customs. Basic attitudes towards life will be established and the foundation of the individual personality established.

This only serves to underline the importance of your creating a rich environment from the very beginning, where good conversation, reading and writing is already taking place. Perhaps it's time to turn off the television and read more for yourself, and with your child. Perhaps it's time to write letters and not simply make telephone calls; to send cards and thank you letters; to enclose first drawings and efforts at mark making in envelopes to send to grandparents, uncles and aunts as messages from your child. Perhaps it's also time to converse with your child rather than instruct and to collaborate using language as the medium, to use rich and marvellous language whenever possible and to sing and rhyme. So much of what your child will learn during this period is done unconsciously, that making a start means starting yourself.

## Developing your child's mind

Studies of the brain have gradually revealed what educators and parents have known instinctively for years: that the experiences children have in the early years of their life have a direct effect on the quantity and quality of connections made in their brain. In addition, there is now evidence to show that, as Dr. Montessori observed many years ago, there are times during this period when the brain is more susceptible to different types of experiences than others, creating what are called 'learning windows', 'windows of opportunity' or 'sensitive periods'.

When Dr. Montessori made her observations of children and responded to what she saw, she had recourse only to words and imagery to try to alert parents and educators to the extraordinary influence that the environment could have upon the formation of a young child's mind. In her book *The Absorbent Mind*, she said,

*It may be said that we (adults) acquire knowledge by using our minds; but the child absorbs knowledge directly into his psychic life....impressions do not merely enter his mind; they form it.*

At no other time have we had more compelling scientific evidence to show us that a child's developing brain is directly dependent upon the quality and quantity of experiences available to her in her early years.

Scientists have also identified the important role that repeated experience plays in the strengthening of these connections. Pathways that are repeatedly used become strong and resilient and continue to refine and develop; those that are not reinforced, wither away around the age of 10, leaving only what is strong and functional to develop.

When you watch your child repeating an action, persevering until she has finished, you will realize that she is doing something far more important than it may appear. So often we cannot understand our child's need to repeat, what to us, appears to be a pointless action, with such fierce determination and concentration. What you are watching, at this moment, is the action of ' life building up'.

## Windows of opportunity

In her observation of children Dr. Montessori pointed out that as a child developed there were certain periods of time which appeared to be the most favourable ones for creating and refining particular human characteristics such as language. She called these special periods, 'sensitive periods' , a term she had borrowed from a biologist. Today the latest research tends to describe them as windows of opportunity. Sensitive periods are important because at no other time in a child's life will she be able to acquire a particular characteristic so easily and well. Once the window of opportunity closes it becomes much more difficult and sometimes impossible for her to acquire these abilities.

The effectiveness of each window relies entirely on the environmental stimuli that a child finds in her environment – in the case of language, the more linguistically rich her environment the greater is the opportunity for development.

Dr. Montessori referred to six sensitive periods that she observed in the young child:

◆ Language
◆ Movement
◆ Socialization
◆ Order
◆ Sensory perception
◆ Fine detail

We shall look at just two of these periods: language and movement.

# The sensitive period for language

The sensitive period for language appears to operate mainly during the first six years of life. During this time your child will naturally focus on those experiences which will best serve this particular window. As a consequence you will see that she naturally focuses her attention on the human voice and is both enthralled and fascinated by it, excited and soothed by it.

From very early on she will focus her attention on your mouth as you speak and observe intently the movements made by your lips as

BELOW **All children experience these sensitive periods. The bold lines below show the window of opportunity that exists for each period. During this time, the experiences offered to a child directly influence the way its mind forms.**

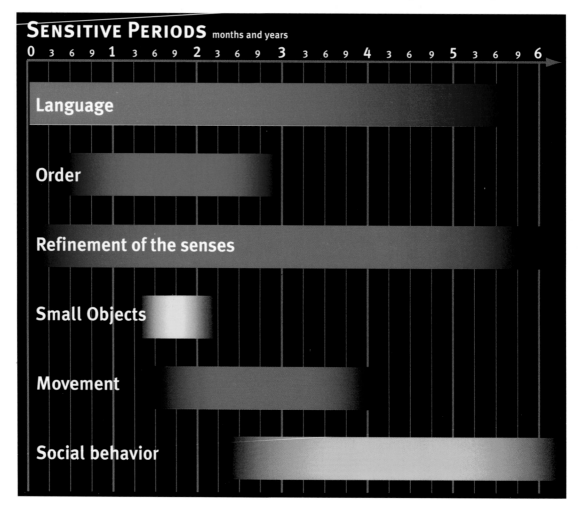

SENSITIVE PERIODS months and years

Language

Order

Refinement of the senses

Small Objects

Movement

Social behavior

well as the sounds produced by them. In each sensitive period there will be a period of internalization before there is any active sign of the characteristic appearing.

Through focus on her language environment your child acquires the ability to reproduce the sounds of her mother tongue with all its nuances, dialects and intonations. The intensity of contact that she makes in the environment is concentrated on language rather than on sounds generally no matter how exposed she is to other sounds: she does not reproduce the whistle of a train or the barking

of a dog instead of language. The ability to learn a second language is highest during this window of opportunity.

All children around the world will produce speech in much the same way, irrespective of the complexity or simplicity of their language – there appears to be a general timetable of readiness that they follow. All the fundamental constructions of language take place before the age of three; just after this age an 'explosion' of d evidence of a real hunger for words, ,nd gradually after that, attention to ,e expands from spoken language to an explo.ation of language in a written form.

### What can you do to help?

One of the easiest things you can do to help is to make sure that you talk to your child from the very beginning of her life. You can engage her in conversation long before she herself has the capacity to understand the precise meaning of your words or before she has the ability to reply. Those close to a child, particularly the main caregivers such as parents, will often wait natural-ly for a response from her which may be given with a little wave of an arm or movement of the lips. Use interesting and varied language when talking to your baby. Tell her what you are doing

and give her the proper names for the things around her – for example, if you are cooking her dinner talk about what you are doing, what you are using and how delicious it will be!

You should sing, rhyme and read to your child as often as possible. Very often children who have an older sibling benefit as they are read to from the moment they are born simply because they are present while you read to your firstborn.

You should make sure your child is included in social situations where she will have the benefit of observing conversation and social

BELOW **Sing songs and recite as many nursery rhymes with your child as you can – it's both enjoyable and an essential part of the process of preparing her to read and write. The better she rhymes the more in tune she is with the patterns of her language.**

interaction. Try to put her in a position, either held in your arms or propped up, to give her a good vantage point where she can see what is happening. Encourage her in conversation. Give her enough time to express herself – children in their early years search for the right words to use to express their ideas and this takes time. If you guess what it is you think she wants to say and get it wrong, she will usually have to start all over again. She may get frustrated around two, when what she wants to say and the vocabulary she has to say it with don't match up. Try to remember that children have a much larger 'passive' vocabulary than an active one, and that they can understand much more than they can say themselves.

Listening to what children have to say gives them a feeling of value and self worth. Being listened to will also encourage them to listen to others too. Listen sensitively to what it is that your child is saying and help her to extend her vocabulary through a gentle questioning process. When you haven't managed to understand what she is saying you may have to ask, 'Did you mean ... or did you mean ...'. In searching for the correct interpretation, you give the message to her that you are trying to understand what she is saying to you, and at the same time you are helping her to hear how she could have expressed herself. If she says something that could have been expressed differently don't correct her – simply provide a 'model by means of confirmation'. For example 'Me like milk – no'! You may reply, 'Ah, you don't like milk'. Remember you are a role model for your child: if you want her to read, you should read, if you want her to write, she needs to see you doing so too.

### First steps to acquiring language

Having focused on the fact that there is a window of opportunity for the development of language, let's look at what language is and how your child acquires it – having an understanding of this will help you to provide the appropriate stimulation for her.

Language is the unique possession of the human being – it is impossible to conceive of any human society functioning without language. Human language is primarily creative and produces new forms of itself continually if required.

We use language for two basic functions: it helps us to communicate with one another, establishing and maintaining social relations, and it provides a system of symbols and patterns that aid our thinking processes. This is advantageous as well as being in its own way limiting. The advantage is that language can help to structure experience – this is especially noticeable when, in the Montessori context, children are helped to identify problems themselves and to work out answers to their questions. Language can also determine the way we perceive things. This can be both helpful, by clarifying concepts and by creating a new level of thinking, or it can be a limitation, for it requires intellectual effort to see things in any other way than our language suggests.

Your child's mind is being formed at a rapid rate in her early years and what is clear is that the quality and quantity of connections made depend upon impressions of the world received through her senses, reinforced through activity and repetition. It is what she experiences for herself in the 'real' world that will shape her mind for the future.

## The sensitive period for movement

The window of opportunity for developing movement, by which we mean physical co-ordination, appears to begin shortly after birth when basic motor skills are developed and the window for refinement of these skills seems to begin around 18 months. The maximum period of development seems to take place in the first four years of life. Giving your child as many possibilities for development in this area in these early years will therefore pay dividends.

It is through movement that your child's personality expresses itself. The more co-ordinated her mind and body are the better able she will be to bring into reality the thoughts and feelings that she has.

There are many reasons why you should help your child develop good co-ordination.
◆ When reading and writing she requires a knowledge of the world – without it she will be at a disadvantage when it comes to interpreting books and may be stuck for ideas when she comes to write.
◆ If she has developed good fine hand control she will find it easier to turn the pages of a book, control a pencil, illustrate and so on.
◆ Increasing your child's independence through her own activity will give her self-confidence. She will know that, generally speaking in her life, she is able to tackle things on her own and be relatively successful. She will be more likely to 'have a go' at things and to have had plenty of practice at solving problems, all of which will help develop some of the attitudes that are helpful if she is to become a reader and an author.

If your child has gained control over her physical co-ordination, she will find it easier to sit and do things – some children find it very difficult to keep their bodies still or to sit, and this hampers their ability to give attention to a task or activity. You cannot force her to be still; it is impossible. What you can do is to help her to gain enough control over her body to allow her to 'will' it to be still. This requires lots of opportunities for games and activities that will bring greater control to her movements.

Your child needs to be outside playing games as much as possible so that she learns to move in increasingly well co-ordinated ways. Taking her into the park, going for walks and letting her explore as much as she is able to will contribute greatly to her development. Games such as Grandmother's Footsteps, Statues, Traffic Lights and 'What's the time Mr. Wolf ?' all help. Developing ball skills, the ability to skip, hop and run should also all be considered vital to her development.

Since co-ordinated movement is a result of experience in the environment you will need to understand that, as much as possible, your child needs to be helped to do things for herself. Although in the beginning this will mean that you will need to invest more time in helping her, once she can do things for herself and in her own time everyone will be pleased.

You should try to prepare your home so that she can explore it in safety and in relative freedom. It is worth remembering that she learns to control her movements through being active herself: showing her how to do things will have a more positive effect than stopping her from doing things. And you will find that it is easier for 'no' to mean 'no' when you are not using it all the time.

For example, give her a small jug with a small amount of juice in it so that she can pour her own drink. This will give her the ability to use her hands with judgement and with little drama should she spill some in the beginning. Developing this small skill will mean that eventually she can help herself to a drink when necessary, put milk on her cereal in the morning, or water plants – or in fact do anything that requires that particular level of motor co-ordination. Helping her to toilet and feed herself, to dress herself, in fact to do almost everything that is helpful for a small human being to know, will also help her refine the control that she has over her body: it's much quicker to put her shoes on than to help her to do it for herself, but once she can do it you are

A boat at sea in the rain

not needed unless she is feeling tired or in need of help.

The more independent your child becomes the more she will be able to participate in life and the more you will find that she will have a positive attitude to all its challenges.

Developing a good ability to communicate and to move with control will greatly enhance her abilities to act independently and to explore

ABOVE **Don't be afraid to let your child do as much as she wants to for herself – even pouring her own milk at breakfast! The better her general hand control is, the better her writing will be.**

the world in which she lives. You will notice that she has a strong urge to do things as you do, for parents are, of course, the natural educators of their children.

# Developing language

### 0 – 8 weeks
Watches the mouth of the speaker intently. Makes mainly biological noises – breathing, eating and those that will reflect hunger or pain.

### 8 – 20 weeks
Good social response to sound of familiar voices. Coos, smiles, enjoys singing, chuckles. May turn head to find source of voices. A variety of sounds made, many sounds being produced.

### 5 – 8 months
Vocalizes tunefully, begins to put syllables together, repeats a variety of sounds. Goo, gaa, muh. Responds to tone of speaker's voice. Gradually over a period of 24-50 weeks the range of sounds become more specific to those uttered in the particular language of your child.

### 8 – 12 months
Uses sounds to communicate with others, babbles tunefully to self and others. Understands the sense conveyed in language and can begin to respond to show that she understands. Can sign 'goodbye' 'hello' etc.

### 12 months
Starts to use words intentionally. Shows understanding of what is said. 'Where is your hat'? 'Bath time'. Can hand known objects to the speaker on request.

### 12 – 18 months
Uses simple words to convey sentences. 'Dada' could mean, Come dad, Dad where are you? There you are. Sometimes it is the intonation that will convey the full meaning.

### 18 – 24 months
Loves nursery rhymes, books, likes to sing. Moves from possible 6 – 20 words to simple sentences and vocabulary around 24 months. Wants to know the names of things and will point and ask, 'What's dat'? 'Why'?

ABOVE **Make books easily available at home so that your child and her friends can discover them together.**

### 2 – 3 years
Loves to be read to. Enjoys rhymes and poems, has favourites. Many sounds still not pronounced accurately but huge increase in vocabulary and complexity of sentence structure. All basic language structures in place. Refinement and expansion now possible. Talks to self while playing and to others.

### 3 – 4 years
Able to use language to convey more abstract thoughts such as likes, dislikes, bad dreams etc. Can speak logically and grammatically, tells stories and continues to expand vocabulary. Likes nonsense rhymes and jokes, and sound games.

### 4 – 5 years
Uses language to co-ordinate activity with other children while playing. Begins to use language in more abstract forms such as writing.

### 5 – 6 years
Asks the meaning of abstract words and uses them. Can use language to describe future and past events. Very clear on tomorrow, next week etc. Precise about age, address, telephone number. Loves jokes. Most grammatical structure is complete by this time. Enjoys listening to stories and 'reading' them.

# Developing co-ordination

### 0 – 8 weeks
Head lags when pulled to sit but gradually develops control as an object may be visually tracked, or turns to the sound of a voice.

### 8 – 12 weeks
Head and chest are held off the floor when lying on stomach. When lying on back enjoys watching and will begin to play with hands. May begin to co-ordinate hand and eyes. Reaching for interesting mobile.

### 12 – 24 weeks
Will learn to roll over. When pulled to sitting keeps head firm. Once sitting the hands are free to 'play' and so needs stimulating objects that are close enough to pick up: a wooden egg and eggcup and a soft knitted ball are useful. Can pass toys back and forth between hands.

### 6 – 9 months
Becomes more able to sit sturdily. Likes to play. Tries to crawl. Loves to poke things with little fingers. Uses one hand to reach for toys, beginning to use fingers. May begin to pull herself to standing position if there is a handy heavy stool or chair to use. Legs seem to practise bouncing in this position. Feeding herself using fingers and spoon.

### 9 – 12 months
Enjoys crawling. Will attempt to crawl upstairs. Will practise standing and letting go so that she lands on her bottom with a gentle bump. Gradually tries standing without holding on. Fingers becoming able to manipulate objects well. Can use thumb and two forefingers to manipulate toys. Uses household objects for their own purpose, for instance will use brush on hair.

### 12 – 15 months
Practises walking and therefore hands free to experiment on the home environment! Is beginning to build objects. Enjoys books and likes to point at pictures. Enjoys holding a crayon and moving it across paper.

### 15 – 18 months
Enjoys moving things that require strength. Can walk up and down stairs with a little help. Likes to be busy with things in the home. Will help unload washing machine. Likes to fetch books and will try and turn pages. Begins to practise running.

### 18 – 24 months
Exploring environment. Wants to take part in life. To dress herself, to toilet herself, to eat for herself. Likes to hold pencil or crayon and make marks on paper – usually circles, lines and dots. Preferred hand often used for picking things up. Wants real work to do.

### 2 – 3 years
Likes to climb. Enjoys cycling on small bike. Jumps and runs with confidence. Kicks balls. Likes to use hands in increasingly co-ordinated way and uses a variety of tools. Enjoys gardening, cooking, cleaning, washing. Wants to use your tools and do everything herself. Loves finger rhymes.

### 3 – 4 years
Increases large movements through games. Likes to play games that challenge her physically. Has good ball skills and good balance. Climbs further and more confidently. Dances. Uses hands to increase her independence. Relatively fine hand control when using scissors, paintbrushes, pencils. Loves finger rhymes. Loves painting. Enjoys feeling objects. Likes Sandpaper Letters.

### 4 – 5 years
Has learned to skip. Moves with greater rhythm to music. Draws recognizable figures. Enjoys writing, both pretend and real. Can colour outlines quite well and is good at sewing. Is always busy. Likes to practise writing.

### 5 – 6 years
Hand really begins to become the tool of the mind. Your child is busy bringing the hand under ever more perfect control of the mind. Will work on topics of interest for hours providing that the hand is also busy. Perfects letter formation.

# CHAPTER TWO

# Developing a Montessori approach

Although you may think that Montessori education is a method, a word that encapsulates it much better is approach. The Montessori approach embodies an attitude to life and particularly to young children as they grow and develop. It is quite possible to do without specialized Montessori material and still have a Montessori approach; it is also possible to have all the specialized Montessori materials in the world and the wrong approach!

There are many activities in this book, some reflective of the kind of experiences your child would have in a Montessori school and others, mostly games, that will provide extra support and more fun for her as she gains in knowledge and confidence. In all these activities it will be important for you to maintain the right attitude towards her learning. At all times you must remember that you cannot learn for your child, only she can do that! What you need is an approach that helps her to learn for herself, one that makes learning fun. Above all it is important to realize that you helped her to learn to walk, talk, become sociable and so much more, by providing a model for her to copy and learn from. Your child absorbed your model and in her own time practised and mastered it. You never doubted for one moment that she would be able to do all these things, and you never made her feel a failure if she didn't walk or talk following your timescale of expectation.

What follows in this chapter are some of the important principles that reflect the Montessori attitude towards educating children, all of which I hope you will find reflect good common sense.

## Children have the power to educate themselves

Simply living in an environment which contains appropriate experiences and activities helps your child learn, especially in the first six years of her life. What is important is to create the right conditions for learning. Research shows us that children who are relaxed and happy learn much more easily than those who feel stress or tension. Much of what your child can learn will be automatically picked up from you in the way that you go about your everyday life. If you wish your child to read and write, then she should live in an environment in which she sees you reading and writing. In addition, when you do come to give her a 'lesson', it should always be pleasurable and fun in itself and not part of the, 'If you don't do this you won't learn to read' syndrome!

## Children learn best when they do so at their own pace

All human beings learn best when they are able to learn at their own pace. What your child's pace is will depend on many different things: in part it will depend on her being able to use previous experiences to support new ideas,

concepts or skills; in part it will also depend on the time of day, her mood and the interest she brings to the activity. Some things she will learn very quickly and some things will take much longer. You cannot judge her by the rate that she learns at. Fast is not necessarily better, nor can we say that the faster she learns the brighter she is! What counts is that whatever your child learns, she must feel secure in the knowledge she has gained. Following her pace requires you to be aware of her and aware of your own

ABOVE **Children like to do things for themselves. Learning to cope with everyday things like dressing gives them confidence in themselves. Confident children are always ready to embrace challenges.**

expectations. In this way you will be able to slow down or speed up according to her learning patterns. Perhaps you will spend several days exploring something that you thought would take five minutes, and five minutes doing something that you thought would take several days.

The ages attributed to each of the activities in this book are a 'best guess' guide and should be treated as approximate. What is certain is that all of them can be enjoyed and played by children under the age of six.

## Children need to make their own discoveries

Can you remember the last time you made a discovery? No matter how small it was, a great wave of pleasure washed over you. Sometimes it felt as if a light flashed on inside your head. Whatever it is that you now know, you know because you discovered it yourself – it is first-hand experience. You get quite a different feeling if you are about to discover something and someone else helpfully reveals the answer to you! All the effort you put in while you were searching for the answer now seems wasted. You often hear children saying, 'You shouldn't have told me, I was going to say that'! You get a grumpy response rather than a grateful one.

Children love to find out things for themselves. Your job is to try and help them to do so, not to do it for them. It is extremely hard to hold back an answer when to you it's so obvious, but hold back you must and give your child time to make the discovery for herself. The skill is in providing just the right amount of help and no more. The form this 'help' takes will vary: occasionally it may mean that you ask her a few leading questions; sometimes you will need to provide a few extra steps for her to reach her goal; most often you will be required to do nothing other than give her more time and observe her more carefully. Doing that is very hard. So often, as adults, we like children to feel that we are the reason they learn something. This gives us a good feeling but it doesn't help children feel that they have the power to learn and discover things for themselves when it comes to more formal learning. I remember a child of just under five coming up to me and saying:

*Child* Do you know, three times three is nine and that's a square, and three of those is 27 and that's a cube.

*Me* My goodness, how do you know that?

*Child* I don't know how I know, but I do know.

I did, of course, know how he knew, but wouldn't have dreamed of robbing him of his discovery, or of the confidence he had gained 'in the knowing'.

The art is to learn how to lead your child to the brink of discovery, then leave her to it. It may be a discovery you yourself had not thought of yet! In this way children will begin to love learning for its own sake and not feel that learning depends upon adult intervention.

## Children learn when they are interested

If you want your child to get the most out of the games that you will play together, you must be sure she is interested in what you are showing her. The following guidelines will also help.

◆ *Choose the right time of the day.* Games that she already knows and enjoys can be played at almost any time; those that are new, and will need all her attention, should only be played when she is fresh and ready for a challenge.

◆ *Be prepared to stop a game if she is unwilling to play, or becoming frustrated.* You will have many more opportunities to introduce her to it. You need a positive response not a negative one. If you have spent some time preparing the activity it can be difficult to accept that she is not interested when you are dying to show her something new!

◆ *Children are usually interested in things when they can use some knowledge or skill they already have to play the game.* Always try to play a game that builds on previous achievements.

◆ *Without interest there is no effort but without effort there is no interest.* If you play a game with your child that is too easy she will play it once and not bother to play it again; if you play a game with her that is too hard, she will be put off and not play it again either. Getting the amount of challenge just right is quite a skill in the beginning. To do this, it's helpful to assess how much of what you are doing is known and how much is new. For instance, you will need to judge the size of the 'steps' that you take when you move from one activity to another. Knowing your child will help: children who find new things daunting will need to take little steps while those who need a challenge if you are to get their attention need much larger ones!

## Children need to develop concentration

Children need to develop the ability to concentrate – without it, it is very difficult to achieve very much in life. The more we are able to give our full attention to a task the more likely we are to succeed. Concentration is similar to any other skill we possess: the more we practise the better we get. Young children often already have the ability to concentrate and adults often, quite unwittingly, do not help to strengthen it. Before your child can begin to concentrate, she needs to be able to give her full attention to the game or task in hand. Once she is able to do that, providing the challenge is right, she will begin to focus more and more deeply on what she is doing. It is this deeper level of attention that we call concentration.

When your child was a baby, she would often look intently at the page of the book you were reading, or at some object that had attracted her attention. Did you wait until she had changed the focus of her attention, or did you distract her from it? So often, when children are very small we do not consider the fact that they might be concentrating. When your toddler is immersed in a game, do you interrupt her without thinking, talk to her and demand her attention? When she wants our attention we will often ask her to wait until we are finished, when we want hers we often insist on it instantly, no matter what she is doing. In many ways, quite unintentionally, adults disturb the concentration of young children and then worry about it years later when they feel that their children lack it!

There are a number of things that you can do to help.

◆ *Cut down the number of television and video programmes that your child watches.* Television in particular is designed to keep her watching, no matter how boring the programme. It does this by flicking from one thing to the next to keep the audience entertained. It's very difficult for a child to learn to concentrate in this situation. Do not confuse occupation with concentration – they are not the same things at all. In

ABOVE **When reading to your very young child, wait until she has finished looking at the picture before you turn the page. In this way, you will help to nurture her ability to concentrate.**

addition, when your child does watch television, do try to make it a more active experience than it might otherwise be. For instance, talk to her about what is happening and ask her to predict what might happen next. Extend her interest in a programme by doing something practical or creative relating to it afterwards. Don't watch for hours on end. If you have the time to watch television with your child, be brave, turn it off and read her a story instead. Reading her a story will encourage her to create images in her own mind to go with the words. Television limits your child's ability to visualise their own pictures in the mind.

◆ *If you are playing a game, try to have the table or floor clear of other distracting items.* Put on the playing surface only what you would like her to give her attention to. Try not to put on the television or radio as this will make it more difficult for her to focus on what you are doing. Music can be good to have in the background, providing that it forms a gentle backdrop and is not jarring.

◆ *Make sure you have everything you will need to play the game before you start.* Getting up and down to fetch things can be very distracting. If you have other children in the family, it may be wise to make sure they are occupied with something that guarantees that you will not be interrupted.

◆ *When your child is concentrating on an activity, try to avoid interrupting her.* Without realizing it, we can interrupt even by praising at the wrong moment. The result of interruption is often that she will stop what she has been doing. You may also need to ensure that other members of the family do not interrupt her either. You should be aware of this from the early months of her life on.

There are of course times when you are in a hurry or something needs to happen urgently. These moments become the exceptions in your and your child's daily life, and can be accommodated more easily. If you see that she is concentrating on an activity just before you need to go out, give her advance warning of the fact you will be going out soon. Tell her that this will mean she will need to think of stopping what she is doing quite soon.

## Children learn by doing

When children learn they need to be active not passive. They learn far more by doing things for themselves than they do by just watching others. Apart from the times when you are reading to your child, she should be more active than you. In addition, in the first six years of her life, your child learns predominantly through receiving impressions through her senses. The more that there is to see, hear and touch, the better.

## Children need praise and encouragement not treats and stickers

It can be very tempting to offer some kind of trade-off to your child to encourage her to complete a given task. The 'If you do this, I'll do that' kind of blackmail may appear to work, and it often does in the short-term, but it gives her the wrong message: that there is no intrinsic value in the activity and the only reason to do it is to gain a reward at the end. Very often children who do things because there may be a biscuit, chocolate or toy in it for them, do not enjoy the experience and do not learn so well because of it. Children are also expert at bargaining and usually hold more aces up their sleeve than you do, so it's a tricky road to start down. Praise and encouragement are all that's needed. If a task is worth doing, then it should be worth doing for its own sake. If it's not worth

RIGHT **Your child will learn most through her own activity. Try to give her experiences that will awaken all her senses: the more she can touch and see, hear and smell, the better.**

doing, you shouldn't be doing it anyway.

When praising your child beware of simply telling her that everything she does is lovely, brilliant, fantastic etc. Most often children enjoy a real recognition of their effort more than blanket praise. Comments such as:

'You found that quite difficult, but you've managed it'.

'That took a long time, you must feel proud of yourself'.

'I like the way you wrote that "e" – which one do you like best'?

Many years ago a little girl of four brought me a design she had been working on, and asked me what I thought of it. I didn't really know what I thought of it and, playing for time, I asked her what she felt about it. This was her answer: 'Well it's not the best I can do, but it's the best I can do today!' A fantastic judgement, and not one I could have come close to matching.

If your child begins to concentrate on an activity, you will also begin to realize that, with concentration, she will often develop the ability

<u>ABOVE</u> **If you have helped your child to cope positively with accidental spills, she will become resourceful in the way she copes with life's daily challenges!**

to persevere and work things through even when they are difficult. The ability to persevere in an attempt to solve a problem will be a very useful ability for her to acquire, especially when she is engaged in more formal learning activities that may require a little unravelling. If children have had the opportunity to persevere and generally arrive at a good solution, they will have a great deal of confidence when tackling the new and the unknown. They will also not mind so much when things don't work out, or they need to call for assistance. A child who feels that she can generally solve problems is able to take the fact that occasionally she can't in her stride. However, if she believes, before she starts, that she won't be able to manage, she will either not start at all or give up at the first sign of difficulty.

## Mistakes are an opportunity for learning

It is important that children and adults feel at ease when they make a mistake. A mistake or error in judgement is an opportunity for learning something new. If we never make mistakes we don't really push the boundaries of our skills or knowledge and we stay well within the limits of what we know. So often children (and adults) are made to feel silly or stupid when they make a mistake. We carry around with us a fear of making an error even though most are accidental or unavoidable. There are many ways you can help your child develop a friendly relationship with her mistakes.

◆ Even when she is very young, you can cultivate a positive attitude to accidental occurrences. If she spills or drops something, don't tell her off – show her how to clear it up, or clear it up yourself then take the opportunity to show her how to carry or use the object next time. You'll be amazed at how responsive she will be. In addition, you will find that next time she spills or drops something she will know what to do to clear it up.

◆ It can be very irritating when someone else always points out our mistakes. It's much better if we have some possibility of recognizing we have made a mistake before someone else comes along and tells us! Whenever possible, try to have some kind of self-checking mechanism in the games your child plays. In Montessori terms this is called a 'control of error'. There are various ways of providing this self-checking mechanism:

You could prepare a 'finished product' which your child can use to check at the end of a game. For example, if you have a game where she is reading and matching words to pictures, a checking device could be added. Write the appropriate word on the back of the picture or make a second set of pictures with the name attached. These can then be used to check at the end of the game. (See Classified Cards, page 54.)

You could add some kind of colour code to indicate if an activity has been done accurately. For example, when playing the Sound Boxes game (see page 57), you could put matching coloured dots on the bottom of each pair of cylinders.

Occasionally, you could show your child that she could check what she has done by using a reference book. Once she is able to write you will be able to show her how to use a dictionary to check her spelling.

The advantage of helping your child to check herself rather than having you check everything, is that she will gradually develop the ability to ask herself how she thinks she has done and this will develop her ability to make a judgement about her own efforts. Learning to ask the question, 'How have I done?' can be very helpful. When we are faced with becoming the active partner in our own learning we feel more in control of ourselves. Your child will not feel dependent on other people's judgement about her efforts, she will instead be able to judge herself.

Even when there is no means of providing a self-check you can look at things together to see if there is anything that needs attention, rather than pointing out what is wrong straight away.

When children are unafraid of making mistakes they will develop an attitude that allows them to have a go at something even if it looks a little difficult. We know that children who develop this attitude find it easier to read. The reason for this is that they don't mind if they don't get each and every word right; they simply have a go at reading what's in front of them and will quite often make a guess at what an unknown word could be from the various clues they pick up from the rest of the page. Then they check for meaning as they progress on through the sentence. Children who are afraid of making a mistake will often dwell on each and every sound in the word, or simply spend a long time staring at it trying to figure out what it says. And they will do this at the expense of understanding what the words are trying to say. These children will need a lot of help when they start to read and will need their confidence and self esteem boosting.

## Repetition is important in children's learning

As we have seen in the previous chapter, repetition is important in strengthening and reinforcing neural connections. Even without this knowledge we know how important the act of repetition is if we wish to make something our own. To be able to do something well, without a great deal of effort, we need to have practised it. The old adage that 'practice makes perfect' is true. Young children often engage in repeating actions, much to our puzzlement. You can watch your toddler putting something into a box and taking it out over and over again, apparently without purpose. However, if it keeps her attention there is something within her that is being established and worked out that we can only guess at. Encouraging your child to practise will be especially important when it comes to writing. She will want to practise if the practice is made interesting, and she definitely won't want to if what you suggest she does looks boring and pointless. Here are two suggestions:

◆ You can provide a variety of different games that help your child to practise the same skill. For example there are many types of games you can play to reinforce her letter recognition. (See Chapter 4.)

◆ Avoid anything that looks boring. A good rule of thumb is to ask yourself if you find it boring. If you do, then your child probably will too! Don't give her page after page of letters to trace, or dull, boring workbooks or reading primers!

## Children learn best when they have chosen an activity themselves

We all tend to be much better motivated when we choose to do something for ourselves. It's easier to tackle challenging activities because we want to, rather than because we are told to. Helping your child to choose will stand her in good stead later in her life. Choosing is not really an easy thing to do although we often take it for granted that everyone can do it. Think carefully about your friends. Do they all have the ability to make choices, or do some of them find it difficult and try to avoid making them at any cost? It is, of course, easier to say that we had to do something due to force of circumstance or because someone told us to. Children often say they were, 'made to do something'.

If we want to make a choice we must have some knowledge of what the options are before we make it. Without this any choice we make is really made on impulse. For instance, if I need to make a choice between two things and I only understand what one of them actually is I can either opt for the one I know, which keeps me safe, or take a risk and opt for the one I don't know. This is not really choosing – more relying on luck or chance. Equally, if I wish to buy a packet of sweets and find myself in a huge sweet shop it's almost impossible to choose anything. Too much choice usually leaves us feeling we still made the wrong choice, no matter how long we took to decide!

Helping your child to make choices needs to be done slowly and carefully. It can begin by offering her a choice of two 'known' things. You could offer her a choice of socks, dungarees, etc. Show her a green pair and a blue pair and ask her to choose which one to wear. Gradually, over time, she can choose from a much wider selection. Perhaps you could put a selection of clothes you'd be happy for her to choose from into a few drawers or shelves. Don't be caught out by leaving summer things in drawers during the winter! And do be sure that once she has chosen what to wear you don't complain. If you don't want her to wear an orange sweatshirt with pink trousers don't include them as a choice.

There will be many occasions when you will be able to involve your child in making choices. During mealtimes you can ask, 'Would you like to have juice or milk today, cereal or fruit?' 'Shall we do some drawing or shall we learn more of those letters today'? Gradually she will develop the ability to make really good choices as she practises weighing up the pros and cons of many different situations.

Very often, offering your child a choice of activity, clothing or food cuts down the number of times you enter into confrontation with each other.

◆ Keep an area such as a shelf or table ready

ABOVE **Helping to sort and organize her clothes will help your child to become aware of the choices that she has each morning when she gets dressed.**

RIGHT **Make sure that your child feels comfortable when she comes to draw and later to write. A table and chair that allow her feet to touch the ground and her arms to be at the right height, are best.**

with all the things that your child might need. The shelf could have a variety of games, pencils, paper etc. Put the current activities that you are using out, making sure that she can reach the shelf herself. Try to keep the things she uses regularly in the same place so that she can always find them. In this way she will be able to choose for herself what she would like to do and when she would like to do it. If possible – and this is rather an expensive option – try to let her have a small table and stool of her very own.

◆ Take time to check that everything on the shelf is complete. Children like to be able to get on with what they have chosen, and if something is missing they may be diverted from practising or playing the game altogether.

One additional way of helping your child to make choices is to ensure that whatever she chooses to do has a reasonable chance of success. If she chooses something that works out well, she will feel more like choosing again. If what she chose was unsuccessful she will feel less like choosing again. That's not to say that all choices should have favourable outcomes, but it is wise in the beginning to limit choices to those activities that are within her reach rather than those that are impossibly difficult.

## Learn to observe your child

Knowing what to show your child next, knowing when she needs practice, when she needs praise, when she needs a challenge, all these things rely on your knowledge of your child. Observing her is essential if you wish to give her the right help at the right time. Perhaps this skill alone is the art of a good teacher: to know what assistance to give, when to give it and how to give it. The following guidelines will help.

◆ Try not to let your child know that you are watching her. When people feel watched they do not usually behave naturally. Develop the skill of looking out of the corner of your eye.

◆ Try to watch out for small details rather than the more obvious things. If you are watching your child drawing, rather than concentrating on what she is drawing, concentrate on how she is drawing. Observe how she holds her

pencil, which movements seem to come most easily to her, which ones she might need extra practice with, whether the paper is in the right position, whether her body is relaxed. Note the time. Does she like to do this kind of activity at this time every day? If so, would it be a good moment to introduce similar activities that may provide more experience in handling writing tools?

◆ If she finds something difficult to do, try and isolate exactly what it is that is causing her a problem. If your child always seems to spill milk when she pours herself a drink from a jug you need to judge the following. Is it because:

The jug is too full.

The jug is too large.

She fails to centre the lip of the jug over the mouth of the glass.

She starts pouring before she centres the lip of the jug.

She moves the jug before it is returned to upright.

She pours too fast.

She doesn't hold the jug securely.

She rests the jug on the rim of the glass.

Lastly, does the jug actually work? Many of them seem to be designed not to pour without dripping!

Learning to observe which of the above is causing the problem means you are halfway to solving it; the other half is solved when you show your child how to master the part that is causing the difficulty.

It can also be helpful to observe situations that cause your child to react in a particular way. Learning to recognize what leads her to enjoy or dislike an activity can be very useful. Different children have different space requirements. Some like to work almost on top of other people while others prefer to keep quite a distance between themselves and others; some are quite happy to work in a confined area and others need to spread out.

Learning to observe your child will enable you to become even more sensitive than you already are to her needs, her likes and dislikes, and to the way she reacts and interacts with others. You will sense when she is ready to learn something new and when she needs reassurance and a chance to repeat what she already knows quite well. It's well worth remembering the old saying that 'Childhood is a journey, not a race'.

## An approach to reading and writing

Before beginning to prepare your child to read and write there are a few other pieces of information that will be useful for you to know about the Montessori approach. Knowing them will help you adapt any of the activities in this book, and any others that you come across, to your particular child without losing the integrity of the approach.

Reading and writing are both complex activities that require a child to develop many different skills and abilities, and to use them all in concert. It is better to master each skill, one by one, especially if the skill is easy to learn because it belongs to a game that's fun to play, whether you are learning to read and write or not. It is very important to play each of the games in this book for its own sake and not as part of a long, never-ending slog towards learning to read or write. You may know that each activity you show your child will help her to do these things, but you don't need to tell her that! One day using all the skills and abilities that you have helped her to build, she should just find herself able to read and write

spontaneously, as you will see in Chapter 4.

To help your child overcome one difficulty at a time you will play games that make use of things that she can already do and which encompass only one new skill or ability. In this way she can progress from something she knows to something that is new in small, attainable steps. Should she need more help, you should simply make the steps smaller and if she finds things too easy you might find yourself taking two or three steps at a time. The important thing is to follow her lead.

To begin to judge the different steps you need to take to prepare your child to read and write, look at both of these complex activities and try to assess all the different skills, abilities and strategies she may need to accomplish them. In doing this you will be able to develop these skills in advance of when they will be needed, helping her to practise them for their own sake. She will love playing the games in an atmosphere of fun, under no pressure to produce an end result.

## Skills and abilities required for reading and writing

### Your child will need

◆ To love and enjoy books so that she wants to learn to read and write.
◆ To have a knowledge of the world around her so that she can make sense of the books you read to her, and use this knowledge to express herself in writing.
◆ To have the ability to use her own language well and to enjoy the sounds, rhymes and patterns in it, as this is the starting point for both reading and writing.
◆ To develop a knowledge of print and how it is used in both reading and writing.
◆ To develop good control over her body, and in particular her hand, if she is to find writing

relatively easy.

## Specifically she will need

◆ To be able to link the sounds of her language to letters of the alphabet.
◆ To be able to write these letters.
◆ To use her knowledge of the world and of her language to extract meaning from written text and to give meaning to her own writing.
◆ To use a variety of strategies to recognize words, sometimes instantly through their pattern or her familiarity with them, or through her ability to work them out.

## Finally, once she can read and write, she will need

◆ To explore how language is used to effect to convey meaning.
◆ To discover accurate ways of spelling words based on regular and irregular patterns.
◆ To explore through her own writing and reading the different forms that text can take, i.e. stories of fact and fiction, poems, letters, diary entries, reference books and so on.
◆ To explore the use of punctuation as a means of helping both reading and writing to become more expressive.

Throughout this book you will find activities to support all these strands of learning, and each of them builds one upon the other until they all combine to contribute to the reading and writing that your child can do.

Although there has been a vast amount of research in the fields of reading and writing, we are still somewhat in the dark as to how it all comes together. Increasingly there seems to be some support for children being encouraged to learn how to read through their own writing, and this approach is one that Montessori schools for children under the age of six have followed since they were founded. Dr. Montessori was probably the first educationalist to suggest that a child, with sufficient knowledge of letter–sound correspondence, would find it easier to write down her own thoughts as a first step rather than read the thoughts of others. She said in *The Discovery of the Child:*

*Writing is developed in the small child easily and spontaneously, in the same way as speech, which is also a motor translation of sounds which are heard. On the other hand, reading forms part of abstract intellectual culture which is the interpretation of ideas represented by graphic symbols, and is acquired only much later.*

However, it is worth noting that she also suggests that children who do not have good hand-eye co-ordination may prefer to read first because they may find the act of writing too onerous. What is certain is that both writing and reading are fused together in a kind of dance, the presence of one enhancing the other.

To understand how it is possible

**LEFT Help your child at the right time and in the right way and he will enjoy discovering the different ways that words can be spelled.**

## Writing

When we write, we start with something that we want to write. We start with something that we know.

In order to write we think of a word and analyse it into its sound components.

For each of the sound components we attribute a letter and either write it or use some other means to represent it, such as a computer, loose alphabet letters etc.

## Reading

When we read, we look at text that has been written by someone else. We start with something unknown.

In order to read we look at the print and try to figure out what the word is. We may do this by letter – sound correspondence, which we must then fuse together by recognizing the word as a whole or by guesswork.

Having identified the word we must cast back and forth in our minds to give it a meaning, and this will depend on our own experiences, the context in which the word appears and the role it plays in the sentence.

---

for writing to precede reading we could look at a simple version of the two processes.

Writing using this model appears to be closer to spoken language than to reading, and more immediately accessible. From a child's point of view, listening to the sounds she hears in her head and working out which letter she will need for each sound requires only a little additional knowledge. In these very early days young children are not concerned with accurate spelling and many do not particularly care whether you can read what they have written or not. (You will soon get used to trans-lating what they have written.) They are justifiably proud of the fact they can write and that seems enough.

Having begun to analyze words into their component parts, it is a very short step for your child to read what she has written. She will do this partly from memory and partly from a growing awareness of the way that she has made the word in the first place.

Throughout the book you will find activi-ties that require your child to acquire specific information: the name of an object, the shape and sound of a letter, the recognition of a word.

When we need to help children to associate a name and an object together in a Montessori classroom, we follow a procedure which we call The Three Period Lesson (it is so called because the lesson falls into three distinct stages). The amount of time spent on each period will depend on your child – usually, however, most time is devoted to the second stage since this is when the child practises associating the object and name together. It is a simple procedure, which can be applied to almost anything once you have mastered it.

## The three period lesson

Usually about three different objects are intro-duced during the lesson.

### Stage 1

Place one of the objects in front of your child and say its name clearly. Do the same for each of the other two objects.

This stage is characterized by the words *This is a .....*

### Stage 2

Place all three objects together and ask for one

of them by name. Once your child has identified the object you want, mix all three up together and ask for another one. Repeat this until she is able to identify the objects swiftly when you ask for them. Encourage her to repeat the name of the object after you from time to time, but don't at this point ask her to try to remember the name. Keep this stage interesting and fun by varying the requests you make, and keep them short so that her attention is not distracted by the command.

This stage is characterized by the words *Give me the..., Show me the..., Put the ..., Hold the..., Touch the..., Point to the....*

## Stage 3

Point to one of the objects and ask your child if she knows its name. Do the same for the other two objects. Repeat this step a few times until she is really convinced that she does know the names of the objects.

This stage is characterized by the words *What is this? Do you know what this is?*

The lesson follows a logical process, which helps children associate objects and ideas and, through a more flexible application, it can also be used to great effect in learning any new knowledge.

The **first stage** clearly sets out the parameters of what is to be learned.

The **second stage** gives your child time to actively connect the new information to her own experience. If you don't give this phase long enough she may not have had enough time to gain the new knowledge. If she is unable to remember the names of the objects during the third phase, this usually means she has not spent enough time learning them properly in the second phase.

The **third stage** helps your child to identify what she now knows that she didn't know before. To know that you know gives confidence. When we are secure in our knowledge

we tend to use it as a springboard for further exploration – your child may use her new knowledge to extend her ideas and experiences in ways that you haven't yet thought of!

Should your child not be able to tell you in the last stage what she has learned, or if she gets very muddled in the second stage, don't worry – simply tell her what the object is and bring the lesson to a pleasant close. It doesn't matter! You will have many, many more opportunities to try again on a different day. This activity is not a test that must be passed; it's simply a very good way of helping children learn particular concepts.

## Following the developmental route

Before we move on to the next chapter, it's worth remembering that what follows works because it takes account of the natural development of your child.

◆ The tremendous power of a mind that appears to be limitless in the amount that it can take on board, particularly through sensory impressions.

◆ Periods of sensitivity that relate to specific developments in the way that a child's mind is formed. In particular, sensitivities to language, movement, order, social development and the development of perception through sensory experiences.

◆ A strong urge for independence.

◆ A desire to communicate.

◆ A strong desire to find purposeful activity or 'work'.

All of these can be nurtured in a loving and supportive environment, an environment in which adults must recognize that, if they are to be successful in helping their child to learn to read and write, they must follow the lead of their child. She is unique on this earth, someone who has never been before nor ever will be again.

# Preparing the way

As you prepare your child to read and write, your role will be rather like that of a conductor rehearsing an orchestra for a concert. She will need to draw on many different pieces of knowledge, and in order to do so, you will need to help her interpret and slot the disparate pieces together in the correct way so that she can succeed.

As a parent you have a unique advantage over teachers. You are a natural educator and you have a very special relationship with your child. You know her in a way that a teacher can never do: you understand her interests and humour. You have times when you can be together without the distraction of other children and without a timetable to follow. You know that your child is marvellous and all children thrive in an atmosphere of love and encouragement.

Pablo Casals in *Joys and Sorrows* expressed it well:

*Each second we live is a new and unique moment of our universe, a moment that never was before and never will be again. And what do we teach our children in school? We teach them that two and two make four and that Paris is the capital of France. We should say to them: Do you know what you are: You are a marvel. You are unique. In all the world there is no other child exactly like you. And look at your body — what a wonder it is! Your legs, your arms, your cunning fingers, the way you move! You may become a Shakespeare, a Michelangelo, a Beethoven. You have the capacity for anything. Yes, you are a marvel.*

From the very beginning of life your child has learned many things from you, by watching and listening to you, by being with you and by sharing her life with you. She learned them simply by living. You can help prepare her for reading and writing in the same way.

## What makes children want to read and write?

Your child will want to read and write if she sees that you enjoy reading and writing. Just as she learned to speak because you spoke to her, so she will want to read and write if it is something that she sees that you do. This means that she needs to see you enjoying a good read or writing in the natural course of the day so that she will come to realize it is something enjoyable that you do for yourself. This is not to say that you have to be seen reading only 'good' literature or writing a sonnet! It won't matter to your child what it is that you like reading: magazines, light fiction, nineteenth century novels, comics, poetry or the sports results. Nor will it matter to her what it is you like writing: lists, letters, notes, crosswords, word puzzles, competition entries or poetry. Just seeing you read and write will make all the difference.

The other single most important factor in helping your child to read and write is to read to her. Read whenever you can and whatever you can – but don't read anything boring. Read to her at least once a day and continue to do this for as long as everyone enjoys it. One family I know still reads together and the children are now 12 and 14 years of age respectively!

There are many children and adults in the world who are unable to read and write and, tragically, there are even more who can read and write but never choose to do so. Don't let that be the fate of your child. From the very beginning you need to engender a love of the printed word in all its forms. You need to help create a desire in her to become a reader and a writer, and the best time for this is before the age of six, during the period that is the most formative of their lives.

## Reading at home

Having a book is rather like having a passport that allows you to travel without ever leaving home: it can take you to another country and can transport you either backwards or forwards in time. Books can make you laugh out loud and they can make you sad; they can help you understand more about yourself and more about other people; and they can help you make sense of personal situations or help you discover new facts about the world. Books can also help us to find out things for ourselves – we can have access to everything that has ever been written down should we require it.

### Finding a place to read

You will need to identify at least one place in the house where you will be comfortable enough to read to your child on a regular basis. A comfy sofa or large armchair in the living room is often a convenient place, and it can also be very useful to have a comfortable spot in her bedroom too. Try to have a selection of books close to the place or places you have chosen as your reading spot or spots.

When your child is very young create a small bookshelf at her own height so that she is able to choose books for herself when she wants to read. Children can choose books long before they can walk, so the shelf shouldn't be very high. If you don't have room for a shelf, prop some books on the floor up against the wall, making sure the front cover of each book is visible – it's nearly impossible for children to choose books when they can only see the spine. You'll find that when books are stored with only the spine showing they will tend to end up in a heap on the floor more often than not, because children pull them off the shelf as they hunt for the cover of the book they have in mind. Change the selection of books from time to time, too, making sure that the favourite one at that particular time always remains. Try to have at least one book of poems and rhymes and one factual book on the shelf at any one time. If you display the books, you will have fewer books out than you actually own, but as you change them around you'll soon discover what your child's particular tastes are, which ones she likes and which, for the time being or even for ever, do not appeal.

If you put a little shelf in her bedroom, arrange a few soft cushions, a rug or a bean bag nearby; everyone needs to be comfortable when they read. Some children like to stretch out on the floor to look at books, and all children like to sit on their parent's lap.

### Reading together

Read aloud as often as you possibly can to your child, and at least once a day. Reading a story out loud is a shared experience and it is very important that she feels included. Physical contact is often vital and both of you must be able to look at the book at the same time. Pictures are an important means of engaging her attention and in the beginning they will

help her to visualize what it is that the text is conveying. If you only have one child in the family this is quite easy to do but when you have more than one a certain amount of organization is essential so that no one feels left out.

Reading together has a value that goes beyond the simple experience of reading a book. It is possible that reading together is the only shared activity in a day for busy, working parents and it can help create a special bond between you and your child. It is a very rare occasion that a child will not want to listen to a story!

You can start to read stories to your child shortly after she is born. Younger siblings are often very lucky as they get to listen to stories from birth. As adults we feel a bit strange looking at a book with a child who is not yet talking, but children of any age can appreciate books. In any event, start reading as soon as you feel able to.

Here are a few simple techniques to help your child learn to handle books. Spend a little time practising them with your two-year-old and she will take very good care of her books.

## Turning the pages of a book

Your child will want to begin to turn the pages herself very quickly, so show her how to do it. Children sometimes try to use their whole hand to scrunch up the page and turn it, or they may hold the page close to the spine, which quickly leads to split pages. Show her how to lift the top or bottom corner of the right-hand page between her thumb and index finger then slide the whole hand under the page as you turn it from right to left. Practise this together. Board books, although sturdy, are too thick for the pages to be turned properly so you will need to show her how to do this with ordinary books.

## Carrying a book

Show your child how to carry a book using

ABOVE **Take time to show your child how to turn the pages of a book (or get an older friend to show him). It will foster his love of books, as he sees exciting new pictures emerge each time he turns the page**

two hands to grasp both sides firmly. Children will often hold only the front or back cover, causing the rest of the pages to flap about.

## Learning to put a book back on the shelf

If your books are propped up with the cover facing outwards you will need to show her how to put the base of the book further out than the wall, then tilt the top edge of the book back on to the wall. If you have books' spines outwards on a shelf you can show her how to make room for the book before trying to slot it into place. This avoids one book being forced on top of another.

With experience, your toddler will get to know which way up a book goes, how to turn the pages and in which direction they should turn, and how to return it all by herself to the shelf.

When your child begins to go off by herself and choose a book, gets comfortable and starts to look through it in a world of her own, you know that you have succeeded in creating a reader – a child who chooses to read. A child who has knowledge of the pleasures books have to offer. She is a child who understands that the illustrations and print carry a message for her to enjoy. When you see that the book is the right way up, that the content is being studied and that the pages are being turned in the right direction, you know that you have achieved the single most important step in helping her to read and write.

## Choosing a book

When choosing books for your child remember that a loved book is one that you will read many times over. It is important that you are not bored by it, as she will ask for it time and time again. If the story, or the pictures, seem lifeless or dull give the book away to someone who may appreciate it! If the book is a gift don't feel badly about putting it away for later, probably much later. Your child needs to listen to books that you value and love; never read a book out of duty. Trust your own judgement – if you think a book is boring, it probably is.

There is nothing wrong with telling your child that there are some books that do not appeal to you or books you feel are not well written. I have a real aversion for the sugary sweet, slimmed-down versions of children's classics that have been re-written in order to cash in on the latest cartoon release. They seem to me to be very badly written, lacking in any real emotional content and often inaccurate. My children, on the other hand, quite like the pictures because they recognize them from the cartoon and all the other merchandising spin-offs they find in every shop. I would rather read the original versions to them when they are a little older.

Because children enjoy the same book over and over again they very quickly remember all the words. If you are reading last thing at night to your child, do not be tempted to paraphrase a book because you are anxious to get to the end. Nor should you attempt to miss out certain pages to get it over and done with. If you do you will have to rely on your memory every time you read the story again. Worse still, if your partner takes over the reading for one night he or she will discover that the version your child wants to hear bears little actual relation to the story in the book!

Be clear before you begin how much you are going to read. With small children the stories tend to be quite short and you can decide together whether you read one or two. Once you are reading books with chapters, you will have to agree on the number of chapters you will read per night. Your child will always want to hear just one more chapter and you can explain to her that this is a sign that the book is written by a very good author. The only other hazard you have to avoid when reading to your child at night is falling asleep before she does, and there are no tips that I can recommend to help you avoid doing that!

As your child grows older and really begins to listen to the words of the story, look at the printed words on the page and ask her open-ended questions about what she thinks might happen and what she believes the characters might be thinking. This will encourage her to give active attention to the story, and active participation of this kind has been shown to have a good effect on reading ability in young children.

It's also good to discuss the meaning of some words as you come to them so that she understands both the meaning and the look of the word.

When words are repeated as part of the repetition of the story, let your child begin to help you say them. This is especially easy if the words rhyme.

## Developing a love of the way language works in books

As you read to your child over the years, she will develop an understanding of the way language is used in stories and the form which stories take. Book language is very different from spoken language and has its own rhythms and styles. Children soon begin to realize that a story begins with words that set the scene and build anticipation, words such as 'Once upon a time', and 'Long ago', are favourites for older children, while often for younger children a more direct introduction is made. They also begin to understand how a story ends: that there is always some kind of resolution, the equivalent of 'and they all lived happily ever after' or simply 'the end'. Writers use many other ways to help them predict what is coming next and children grasp all of them as they are read to. In reading stories written by six-year-olds, I notice that many of them seem to start with 'One day' and all are brought to a conclusion, sometimes very abruptly!

Book language is much more descriptive and more rhythmical than spoken language. A good book will help your child, through its use of words build vivid pictures in her mind. When in speech would you ever say the following, from *The Whales' Song* by Dyan Sheldon and Gary Blythe?

*Lilly's grandmother told her a story.*

*'Once upon a time', she said, 'the ocean was filled with whales. They were as big as the hills. They were as peaceful as the moon. They were the most wondrous creatures you could ever imagine'.*

Early books can also give children experiences that will help them to move on to more complex forms of books as they mature.

The author Mem Fox describes how in her book *Possum Magic* she deliberately begins with, 'Once upon a time...' in order to link it to all the stories children will have heard before they read her story, and those stories that will come after. She also makes *Possum Magic* an archetypal quest story, in preparation for the many quest stories that children will meet in the future, such as Homer's *Odyssey* and the Arthurian legends.

It is worth mentioning that children also like the sensations that a book offers. The size of a book, the smell of it, the type of paper that the book is printed on, the illustrations, all these elements play their part. There is no doubt that some books make a deeper impression on children than others, and in part this can be due to the fact that more senses have been aroused by these books than just the ear and the eye.

## The importance of illustration

Illustrations play an enormously important role as your child listens to you read and begins to read herself. Good illustrations will help her to work out what is happening in the story. The younger your child is the more vital the pictures are: it is very often the pictures that first fix her attention on a book, and she will use them to help her to predict what the story line is. Helpful illustrations will clearly show what is happening in the text. Long before your child can read she will sit down with a book, study the pictures and use them as a way of 'reading' the story. It is possible to see children as young as 18 months doing this and by around the age of two you will sometimes hear them telling a story to go alongside the pictures.

RIGHT **Book illustration should be inspiring and absorbing – like this one from *The Whale's Song* by Dyan Sheldon and Gary Blythe. Pay as much attention to the quality of the illustration as you do to the text.**

There are many very good picture books for young children – some use photographs and some illustrations. Try to find some that tell a story using pictures only, then your child can help you to tell the story and also 'read' it to herself and others.

Illustrations can also inspire children to create artwork of their own, so it's a good idea to choose books with beautiful examples of different techniques. I'm not in the least artistic but many have appealed both to me and the children that I have known, and I have listed them later in this book, in Chapter 9.

## Art activities

You can use a good book illustration as a model for your child to look at to create her own picture – all you'll need to supply is some paper and pencils (preferably in lots of jolly colours), or a small blackboard and chalks. The fact that you have chosen an illustration from a book to act as your inspiration may in turn inspire her to tell her own stories using pictures alone. She may also decide to draw and put her own words to her artwork. Depending on her ability to write, you may write down words as she dictates them, she may put 'marks' on her own illustration or she may write a few words or a whole story to go with it.

In some books the illustrations tell the story in more detail than the words, and these can be particular fun for your young child. For example in the classic book by Pat Hutchins, *Rosie's Walk* , the story very simply tells us of Rosie's walk home through the farmyard to the hen house. The humour of the story lies with illustrations which show the disastrous attempts of the fox to catch Rosie as she walks on, oblivious to his presence. The text never once mentions the presence of the fox. Children love the jokes contained in the sub-text of the pictures, and after one or two pictures are able to anticipate the fate of the fox.

## A guide to the content of children's books

To help you to get to know the range of books available for young children I would recommend that you join your local library. Librarians are trained to know what is available for young children and should be able to suggest titles for your child that will revolve around her interests; they also have access to all the latest titles. Libraries also sometimes have story-telling sessions for young children, and other events that revolve around books, all of which can be fun to attend. When your child is around three she can have her own library card.

Recent studies show that children seem to benefit most from text that is slightly more complex than their own speech, and that they love to hear more complex vocabulary than they can themselves use.

A good rule of thumb to follow is that the younger the child, the more realistic the content should be. Try to limit the more fantastic and grotesque stories until your child is six or over – many of the traditional Brothers Grimm or Hans Christian Anderson fairy tales are more appreciated when a child has a firm grip on the difference between fantasy and reality. Your child herself will give you clear indications of her understanding of the differences between the two. Around the age of four most children will start to tell you the difference between something that is pretend and something that is real. My own children identified the difference by adding the words 'in true life' when they were speaking of something that really had or could happen. Around the age of six, children clearly start to enjoy the tensions that come with suspense and adventure and have a really good feel for the ridiculous. They are also ready to appreciate the 'rightness' or 'wrongness' of human actions at this age and can put themselves into the position of others, so they are ready for this kind of literature.

Choose content for your child that is life affirming and that helps her to explore the many different facets of her world and extend her understanding of it. Repetition and rhyme are also important factors in choosing books that appeal to this age group.

What follows is a rough guide to the type of content that children may be interested in according to their age. There is a fuller list of books you may find useful later in the book, in Chapter 9.

### Up to Two

Very young children will want to go backwards as often as they want to go forwards when they look at a book. The pictures will catch their attention. This is absolutely fine in the early stages as they need time to comprehend that a story has a beginning, middle and end.

Try to follow your child's interest, although storytelling at this stage is not easy. Try pointing out familiar things in the illustrations and talking about them, then gradually look at more complex aspects of the drawings. You can attach a little story to the drawings by describing what is happening in them. The next step is to summarize text and eventually you will be able to read the text.

Try to set aside a particular time each day on a regular basis for 'reading' and don't be disappointed if she loses interest quickly. Songs and rhymes will be very popular at this stage, and well-illustrated books which contain those songs and rhymes familiar to your child can be helpful.

Books containing photographs of well known everyday objects and animals can also be of interest at this age. Particularly popular are 'flap' books which reveal all manner of things hiding under the flap. Board books are sturdy and last well, although they can be difficult to manage when your child begins to want to turn the pages.

### Two to Three

Books that expand the range of nursery and poems that they already know are particularly popular with this age group, as are everyday events made into stories. Subject matter that centres on things that happen in and around the home will help your child's sense of security develop as she finds herself able to predict what happens in her life. Look out for books that reflect your environment, whether it be inner city, suburb, countryside, animals, and so on.

You should now be reading stories with a simple plot that will eventually be learned by heart. Don't try and skip any pages!

Remember to look at factual books as well as fictional ones.

### Three to Four

Stories should continue to follow the everyday happenings of your child. At this stage the contents of some of her books should not only support and confirm her knowledge but also stretch it. Try to find accurate, informative books based around your child's interests, as she will now be curious to fill out what she knows with much more detail. Books that deal with emotions are also very helpful for children of this age group, as are those that help her deal with new situations, such as starting preschool, going to the doctor or having a new brother or sister. Humour tends to be enjoyed if it is of the 'slapstick' variety.

### Four to Five

Now your child needs books to help develop her understanding of the world, books that open up windows into other people's lives, how they live and what they do. Stories should be getting longer with more complex story lines, and should have more text than pictures so that they can be read aloud. Provide lots of reference books. You will also need to search for books that she can start to try to read and remember.

She is more likely to read about something she is interested in than something that is easy. Choose books where the language is simple but well written. Humour becomes even more important now than it was before – children are able to identify when something predictable is used in an unpredictable or inappropriate way, and therefore enjoy a more subtle sense of humour. Many poems offer children the chance to appreciate a more humorous view of life and are also excellent for the beginning reader.

### Five to Six

Your child should now be able to enjoy longer books with fewer pictures and more complex plots; you could start to read books that have chapters. She will appreciate books that give instructions on how to make things or do experiments, and an atlas and perhaps a first dictionary could be useful additions to her library. Humorous poetry will be enjoyed, too, particularly where there are subtle word plays which affect the meaning of the subject matter. Books by Roald Dahl are also brilliant for this age group.

## Raising children's awareness of print

Alongside the sheer pleasure of reading to your child, you can take the opportunity to help her to become aware of 'print' itself; the more aware she is of it, the more this knowledge will support her when she comes to read and write.

In drawing her attention to print in the books that you read, try to avoid making reading into a formal teaching experience. And try not to spoil the flow of the story or the special magic of the moment simply to point out, for example, the use of a capital letter!

As always, respond sensitively to your child. If she seems interested in spending some time looking at 'print' then do so; if she is singularly lacking in curiosity about it, save it for another day. You will be reading to her almost every day for at least six years and during this time many of the points below will arise quite naturally.

◆ *Help your child to see which way print goes when you read.* In the Western world children need to know that print is read from left to right and from top to bottom. One of the ways that you can show this is to let your finger run along the page as you read. Only do this from time to time, however, and be careful not to let it interfere with the rhythm and pace of the text as you read. She will soon get irritated if it does!

◆ *Tell her who created the book.* Explain that the author is the person who thought up the story and wrote it down; explain what an illustrator is.

◆ *When you read to your child don't just start where the story starts.* Read the title of the book, then the names of the author and the illustrator. Show her where this information can be found. If there is a dedication, read this and explain to her what a dedication means.

◆ *Do the same with any poetry that you read.* Look at the different layout of the words, check where the title of the poem is written and where the poet's name is.

◆ *Look out for the 'information' pages.* The contents page, chapter headings, page numbers and indexes can all give you a great deal of information about the book.

◆ *Study the words on the page as you read.* If you read a long word find it on the page and have a look at it. If you read a very short word, do the same thing. Ask your child to tell you which of the written words is the long word that you have just read.

◆ *Study the punctuation, looking for only one thing at a time.* Look at full stops/periods and ask what they are for. Find question marks. Ask her to tell you whether all the print on the page looks the same. Point out when capital letters are used after full stops/periods or for names. Ask her how she can tell when someone is speaking.

## Becoming aware of print in the environment

The printed word is found everywhere in our environment. Your child is constantly absorbing all the aspects of the world in which she lives and it will not take her very long to work out that print symbolizes language.

You can help by exploring it with her in the following ways.

◆ *Writing down your child's name is one of the most potent ways of drawing her attention to print.* Use her name in appropriate places around the house, for instance on her bedroom door. Or you can write her name on the refrigerator door in magnetic letters and on special items of clothing. The possibilities are endless.

◆ *Let her cut out all the letters in her name from magazines and newspapers.* This will enable her to notice all the different ways of writing these letters. Let her choose which ones she likes best and glue them down to make her name.

ABOVE **Making your child actively aware of the print in her environment is easy and fun. This little girl can already recognize the different kinds of print her mother has taken from a newspaper and is now cutting up individual letters to glue them on to paper to spell out an important message – her name!**

LEFT **Make use of the many opportunities you have when out and about with your child. Pointing out the labels attached to items as you shop is a great way to learn about print. It doesn't take long for children to recognize the names of their favourite items.**

◆ *Children quickly become aware that print is used to identify things.* Shop names, magazines, foodstuffs and signposts are just a few examples that your child will encounter on a daily basis. As you go out and about with her look at these names and point them out to her. When you are in the supermarket ask her to collect well-known items and use the opportunity to point out the names on the labels.

◆ *Draw or cut out road signs.* Make two sets to play a simple game with your child. Turn all the cards face down and see if you can find pairs by taking it in turns to turn up two cards at a time. The one who gets it right gets to keep the pair; the one who gets it wrong turns her cards face down again.

◆ *Play this version of I spy.* Choose the first letter of your child's name and see how many times you can find things that start with the letter when you are out for a walk. Choose other letters on other days.

◆ *Collect blank forms when you are in the post office or bank.* Keep similar forms that get sent through the post. Your child will have fun filling them in!

Examining print with your child should always be purposeful and part of a wider exploration of language. What you must not, under any circumstances, do is provide 'flashcards' for her to learn by heart. One family I knew attached printed names to all the items of furniture in their house in the hope that, as their toddler bumped into them, she would focus on the printed word and learn it. This is at best sad and a real misconception of the role that the printed word plays in reading.

Print is only valuable if it conveys meaning to your child – learning isolated meaningless words has no value at all. Children do not become readers for the pleasure of decoding words. They can of course, learn to recognize words on paper, and their minds have such

fantastic capacity that they will, if you make them, recognize words taught in this way. But what value do they have? Will they help her choose to read when the time comes or will they simply make her precocious? You will be wasting valuable reading time if your try to teach her in this way. Print conveys meaning and meaning must connect with experience of life to have any value. Knowledge and understanding of the world is of vital importance in your child's conquest of reading and writing.

## Why your child needs knowledge and understanding of the world to help her read and write

Whenever your child reads or is read to she focuses her attention, not on the words themselves, but on the meaning that lies behind the words. Children when they read are in search of meaning. In order for your child to grasp the essence of words, therefore, she must have experiences that correspond to the words that she hears or reads. She does not need to know all there is to know, but she must have enough knowledge to make some sense out of them. No child can give attention to anything for very long that does not hold meaning for her, but where words and knowledge meet there is a wonderful flowering of imagination. This flowering is valuable for children whether they are interpreting words written by someone else or trying to write down their own words. It is in the 'gap' between the words on the paper and your child's own experience that something dynamic and creative occurs. It is in this 'gap' that she is able to reflect upon the resonance between the world that she knows and the world that she is imagining.

What your child will get out of a book will depend very much on what she brings to it. In addition to a general understanding of the world, she will bring her own preferences, tastes, interests, humour and humanity. Who said listening to stories was easy?

You can help by making sure that you take her out and about and give her experiences of the world that she can talk about and have all to herself. Incontrovertible! Take her out at night to look at the stars; sit in the park when the grass has just been mown; listen to the rumble of the trucks as they go down your street; taste lemons. Let your child explore the world through her very own experiences – you can't smell mown grass on television!

## Developing language

Experiences need language and language needs to be precise, varied, flavoursome, structured and rhythmical.

Your child's ability to use spoken language is the foundation upon which all other forms of language will rest. The importance of helping her to develop a good vocabulary cannot be underestimated. Of equal importance is the shaping and structuring of the form language takes, its grammar and syntax. The texture and quality of her language development will depend very largely on the kind of speech that she hears in her social environment.

Children love words, they love the sounds of words and, dare I say, they love the taste of them. They want to know the names for everything that surrounds them. From a very early age they point and ask, 'Wots dat'?, or simply raise the tone of their voice in a question, 'Huh'?

There is no limit to the number of words that your child can take on board, nor is there any limit to the length of words that she can understand. She may not, of course, be able to produce a long word accurately for herself but this does not mean she lacks understanding of its meaning. Recently there has been a suggestion that the size of our adult vocabulary can be predicted by the number of words that filter through us during the first three years of life.

Reciting the dictionary to your child every morning is not, however, going to achieve the desired effect. Words must have meaning, even if the meaning needs refining and developing through experience.

To help you can:
◆ *Use your language creatively and well.* Use different words to describe events, feelings, tastes, in short everything. We sometimes get lazy when we choose words to describe experiences.
◆ *Involve your child in lots of conversation from the earliest days.* Talk through what you are doing. Ask questions. Use questions to build logical thinking. 'What shall we do next'? 'What do we need'? 'How many shall we buy'? I used to tell my three-month-old child that I was going out of the room for a short while and would be back. Although I knew he didn't understand the words, I'm sure he understood the message.
◆ *Give names to new experiences.*
◆ *Play games that support language development.* See pages 52-53 for some ideas.
◆ *Play with language: invent rhymes and poems.* A game I used to play with my children when they were three and four was to use unconventional words to replace name-calling. 'You teapot, you glass of milk, you empty sugar bowl'! When we began, the words we used were always randomly chosen but gradually, as we became better at it, they had to be connected. All their anger very often disappeared in howls of laughter as each child struggled to find more and more bizarre words to hurl at the other.

If your child is reading and is faced with a new word, her mind will automatically select all the meanings that she knows that could be connected to the word. One of these will be chosen as appropriate, based on other clues contained in the sentence. A child with a poor grasp of vocabulary will draw a blank very easily.

Equally, a child who has been used to hearing quite complex sentence structures will use her knowledge to get at the meaning of sentences. Grammatical and syntactical knowledge will help her to predict the meaning of words and unlock the meaning of sentences.

Children's use of language helps in other ways too. Without necessarily having a knowledge of nouns or verbs etc., a child can often predict what kind of word is she is looking for from the place it occupies in the sentence. For example: Rachael dortrand the boat. A child who hasn't come across the word dortrand before will search for words that have some kind of 'action' to them. This is based on her deep knowledge of the particular word order in English: she knows she is hunting for a verb.

Here are some games you can play to help with language development.

## Naming objects

This is like a treasure hunt. You name an object and your child has to find it and bring it to you.

You can choose to ask for interesting objects, such as a corkscrew, ladle, or spaghetti tongs.

## Naming your body

Name all the parts of the body. Don't just stick with the obvious ones. Remember shin, instep, ear-lobe, cheekbone, shoulder blade, calf, etc.

## Simon Says

Once your child has acquired the vocabulary, both of the above games can be played as Simon Says.

It's easy to play: when a command is prefaced by the words 'Simon says', you must obey; when it isn't prefaced by 'Simon says' you must not obey.
Simon says 'Touch your thumb' Child does so.
Simon says 'Bring the milk jug' Child does so.
'Turn your head' Child does not do so.

## Naming the parts of objects

Take a single object and see if you can name all the parts on it. Choose anything that you can stand in front of, for instance a car: radiator, door, wheel, bonnet, driving-wheel, rear-view mirror and so on.

## Guess the object

Age: around 4

### You will need

A large bag or a blindfold. Put several different but familiar objects into the bag if you're using that instead of the blindfold. If you're using the blindfold, put the objects on a table or other surface.

ABOVE **Choose an everyday object such as a door and see how many of its parts you can name. Here you'll find a handle, lock, doorframe, knocker, fan-light, number and panels.**

### How to Play

Your child puts her hands into the bag and describes what she can feel without actually saying the name of the object. You try and guess the name. After a while change places with each other.

Wearing the blindfold makes this game a little simpler, particularly if you put on the blindfold. Your child can look at the object and try to describe what she sees; you have to guess what it is. After a while change places with each other.

## Guess the word

Age: around 4

### How to Play

This is like a very simple game of charades. You can do it with 'actions' to begin with then later you can do it with prepositions.

You act out an action – for instance, hop

Your child guesses what the word is. If she gets it right it's her turn.

You will find that she will automatically choose a verb to name what you are doing. Start with very obvious things then become more subtle as you go along. Other actions you might use are:

*skip, jump, run, smile, laugh, cry, dance, think, sleep.*

To play the game with prepositions, use a couple of toys from your child's collection, or you could act it out yourself using your body and a chair, bed, table or whatever else seems convenient.

Assume you have a small tin and a marble:
*Put the marble in the tin and ask - 'Where is the marble'?*

Your child will say,' In the tin'.

*Put the marble on top of the lid of the tin and ask 'Where is the marble'?*

Your child will say, 'On the tin'.

*Put the marble next to the tin and ask 'Where is the marble'?*

Your child will say, 'Next to the tin', or perhaps they will say, 'Beside the tin'.

Continue until you have exhausted all the possibilities. Take it in turns.

## The question game

Age: about 3 on

This game will help your child to develop relevant vocabulary and logical thought structure around a theme well-known to them. Even though the questions you ask should provoke logical answers, they very often do not. Keeping her on the topic and gathering as much information as you can is quite an achievement. At the end of the questioning period you can weave the information you have gathered into a story.

Choose a simple event that she will have experience of, for example Daddy and Natalie baked a chocolate cake.

Ask her a series of questions around the event to build up as much background as you can. Try to keep everything logical.

If you start by asking questions about the subject – Daddy and Natalie in this case – you should receive information that will be useful for setting the scene.

*Who* is this story all about?
*What* do we know about them?

RIGHT **Playing Guess the Word can involve a lot of activity – even if all you're showing is 'sleep'!**

Move on to ask questions around the verb – in this case baking. This should be useful for gathering information around the action of the story. Now ask for information about the cake.

*Why* were they baking a cake

*How?*

*When?*

*Where?*

*With what?*

*What* kind of cake?

Finally ask some questions that will bring about a conclusion.

*So what happened in the end? How did everyone feel?*

The following game will also help your child to sequence events and tell a story.

### Making a storyboard

Age: about 3 on

**You will need**

Pictures you have cut out of a catalogue, or that you have drawn. You don't need to be an artist, however – you could for instance use photographs of your child during the course of her day: of her getting up, brushing her teeth, getting dressed and so on. The important thing is that the pictures should form a sequence.

**How to Play**

Ask your child to place the pictures in the sequence she thinks they should go into. Once they are in sequence you can make up a story to go with them and she should be able to help you do this.

If you take photographs of your child's day you could make them into a book to create a more permanent record of the story (see Chapter 9 for simple ideas on how to do this). She will enjoy looking through the pictures for many years to come.

You can become quite adventurous in choosing your theme: you could draw the sequence that needs to be followed to make biscuits or flapjacks. Once your child has put them in order, she can stick them down or make a book out of them, and make the biscuits following her own recipe!

## Classifying

Another type of game that helps your child develop a wider vocabulary is one in which you sort and classify objects that belong together. Children organize and order their experiences all the time, along with the words that they learn to describe them with. You can prepare a whole range of pictures or objects that could help them to do this – see Chapter 9 for more ideas.

### Classified cards

Age: around 2 – 2½ on

**You will need**

Collect a set of pictures that belong together. For example, for younger children use pictures of objects from each room in a house; if possible have one card that shows the room as a whole. You could also use pictures of things in a street, in a park, in a supermarket and so on. On the back of each individual picture write the name of the object it contains. For older children you could put together a set of anything that they were interested in: motorbikes, wild animals, garden flowers.

**How to Play**

If your cards are of rooms in a house, start with one room – say the kitchen. Take out the picture that shows the kitchen as a whole. Talk about it. Now show pictures of objects in the kitchen and see how many your child can name. Use the cards as opportunities for discussion. Arrange the cards that she knows under the picture of the whole room. Help her learn the ones she doesn't know using the three period lesson described in Chapter 2 (see pages

37-8). If she looks at a picture of a chopping board and volunteers 'bath mat' use the opportunity to 'classify'. You could ask her whether it was likely that the bath mat would turn up in the kitchen! When she can identify the cards from more than one room, mix them up and see if she can sort the objects into their respective rooms.

If you place a little identification symbol on the back of each set before you play the game, she will be able to check herself whether or not she has sorted the cards correctly.

## Sorting objects

Age: around 2½ on

### You will need

A selection of any items that can be sorted or classified, for instance:

Objects that sink or float

Objects that are magnetic or not

Objects that are hard or soft – feathers, pebbles and so on

Objects that are used for drawing and objects that are used for painting

Objects that are heavy or light

### How to Play

Show your child how to sort out the objects according to the way you have classified them. You can separate the groups on to either side of a table or a plastic mat.

If you want to provide her with a mechanism for self-correction you could draw the objects, in their groups, on a piece of paper.

## The importance of rhyme

Children who have a wide experience of rhyming are known to do well at reading and to have a strong sense of how to spell. The greater your child's awareness of sound and its patterns the better the fit will become between the patterns of letters in words and her ability to predict what it is they say. It is impossible to underestimate the importance that a good knowledge of poems, songs and nursery rhymes will play in helping her to read and write.

Children love the humour and predictability that comes with rhyme and they love the rhythms that it sets up. They also love playing and making rhymes themselves. You should, therefore, have a wide repertoire of nursery rhymes and poems. In the event you find that your memory does not serve you well, there are many good tapes you can buy. Play them and learn them alongside your child; no matter how good a tape is, there is really no substitute for singing or reciting poems and songs yourself with your child.

In addition to focusing on rhyme you can help her to recognize clusters of sounds such as 'str' or 'br', 'ing' or 'ake'.

◆ Play games to see how many words you can think up with 'str' at the beginning.

◆ See how many different words your child can think of that rhyme with, say, cake.

◆ Make sentences using the same sound at the beginning of each word. For instance, Sister Suzie sat singing songs by the seaside.

Poems and rhymes will also provide a wonderful resource for early attempts at writing and reading. Knowing what word should come next will certainly be a great help when your child first begins to read. Poems and songs are also good to write down when you first begin to make words. Poems that have lots of rhyme and repetition help children to pick up the look of the word and that can help them to write relatively accurately when they first start writing words down.

*Man fat*
*Top hat*
*Fell flat*
*Squashed hat*

(Anon)

ABOVE **From the very beginning, help your child to solve problems for himself. In Classified Cards, for instance, he can first sort the cards, then use already identified control cards to check whether his pairings are correct.**

This is a favourite of mine and one that is easy to write.

Rhymes and songs can also teach children the order of the alphabet and it's both fun and instructive to sing them often with your child – you can start doing these as early as possible, from about the age of two on, and continue until they don't want them any more.

## Games with rhyme and rhythm

Chapter 4 has a selection of rhyme games, or you could try the ones given below.

### Clapping game

Clap the rhythm of the words and syllables alongside the poems and songs that you know. Clap the rhythm of all the names of the members of your family.

### The echo game

You clap a rhythm and your child answers back with the same rhythm. An alternative to this game is to collect a number of different objects that would make a sound. Each of you has the same things. Sit back to back. You pick up your (say) chopsticks and tap a rhythm. Your child picks up her chopsticks and echoes you. You pick up your spoon and glass, and tap a different rhythm. Your child has to echo you.

## Games to develop listening skills

Other games can develop children's listening skills – listening plays an important role in developing speech and in helping the ear to become focused on fine differences in sounds. The following games will all help your child to listen, which will later help her to recognize sounds attached to letters.

### The bear and the honeypot

You need at least three people to play this game. One child dons a blindfold and puts a pot (the honeypot) just in front of her. One of the other children (or adults) tries to approach very quietly and take the honeypot. If the blindfolded child hears her, she points and that child or adult has to sit down. Another player then tries to grab the pot. If a player manages to grab the honeypot, the blindfolded player relinquishes the blindfold to her and joins the other players.

### Listening to sounds

Get your child to close her eyes and try to identify what she can hear. Suggest that she focuses on sounds that are far away, then nearby, then inside her body and so on.

### Identifying the sound

Choose a lot of familiar, everyday objects, hide them behind a tray or ask your child to put on a blindfold. Pour water into a glass, crumple a piece of paper, put the lid on a saucepan, drink from a cup etc. Your child has to guess what the sound is.

### A moving sound

Use something that makes a very soft sound – a clock that ticks, sand in a container, a pair of chopsticks. Ask your child to close her eyes and point at the sound while you move around the room with it. You must move very quietly. If your child manages to point at you then it is her turn to make the sound.

### Sound boxes

Age: from about 3½ on

**You will need**

Collect eight identical containers with lids – smartie tubes, plastic pots with lids, used film canisters are all suitable. Nothing should be too large. Make four pairs by putting different substances into each of two containers: sand, sugar, rice, dried beans and macaroni would all work. Identify each pair by putting matching coloured dots on the bottom of the containers. (This will enable her to check whether she has identified the different pairs correctly.)

**How to play**

Separate out the two sets of containers. Now show your child how to shake each container, preferably in each ear, then search for its match.

Help her to remember the sound by putting one set further away, perhaps in the kitchen. Then listen to one container, go to the other set and listen through to see if the same sound can be found.

### Story tapes

Having a book and story tape that match can be very useful, although it's no substitute for direct contact with you. There are many excellent tapes and stories available now and these can be especially useful on car journeys. If your child has a book that she is very fond of, you could actually tape the story yourself.

### Song and rhyme tapes

These can be lovely to listen to, particularly on journeys, and help to expand the range of nursery rhymes and songs that you can sing or say with your child. As your child gets older remember to look out for 'grown up' poetry tapes.

### Sound lotto

There are many good sound games commercially available, such as sound lotto. See Chapter 9 for a list of recommended games.

## Preparing the hand for writing

Before your child can be expected to control her hand sufficiently well to write letters, she must have lots of practice in guiding it. Children need activities that will help them to move their hands ever more precisely and

ABOVE **Everyday objects can be recycled to help your child learn – these used film canisters have been pressed into service for Sound Boxes (page 57), which helps develop listening skills.**

carefully. You can begin these activities from as young as 18 months.

There are many things that you can show her how to do which will give her greater independence. Learning how to pour can be excellent. Having the ability to pour things for herself will allow her to take care of her own needs: she can have a drink when she is thirsty, put milk on her cereal, water plants, pour ingredients into saucepans and do many other things that require that kind of movement. At the same time the more control she gains over her hands the easier it will be for her to control them when she wishes to write.

Try and give your child some pouring to do at home. Begin with something simple then increase the difficulty, one step at a time.

◆ Using two small jugs, put some fairly large beans in one and encourage your child to pour from one jug to the other without spilling any beans. Have the jugs on a tray so that if any do spill they won't go all over the floor.

◆ Using a finer grain such as rice, pour just enough into a jug to fill three egg cups. Now ask your child to pour the rice into the egg cups. If she ends up with extra rice, or runs out of rice, she will know that she needs to try even harder next time. Encourage her to repeat these activities as often as she likes.

◆ You can now do the same activity but using water. Have a cloth nearby so that she can wipe up the water if she spills it.

As soon as she is able to pour, encourage her to use her newfound skill. And by looking around your home you will discover many other, similar skills she could learn, for instance:

◆ Help her to learn how to butter her own sandwiches. Make sure you limit the amount of butter available in the beginning.

◆ Show her how to peel her own fruit.

◆ Show her how to cut up her own fruit. Start with soft fruit such as bananas, and a blunt knife. You will need to demonstrate how a knife is held and carried, then where fingers must be when you use a blade to chop fruit. She will be very serious about this responsibility and very much enjoy being allowed to do something as 'grown up' as cutting fruit.

## Puzzles

Look around for puzzles that have knobs on each of the pieces. These can be very useful because they encourage your child to use her thumb and index finger, which she will

A boat at sea in the rain

**ABOVE** Being able to do things for yourself gives you confidence. Cutting up your own fruit can lead to a greater willingness to have a go at acquiring other new skills, such as reading and writing.

eventually use to control a pencil. The knob becomes the substitute pencil and her hand develops strength and the habit of using only a few fingers to accomplish a task.

## Drawing

Your child will have begun to draw using crayons when she was about 18 months old. The patterns and shapes that she draws naturally are lines and circles. Slowly, however, her art will become more representational. Children will first draw something and give it a name, then decide what they are going to draw and try to represent it. When your child is between four and five you can suggest that she looks at a real object with you, then tries to draw it. This will help her eye focus on a shape and direct her hand to try and represent it.

## Writing patterns

Incorporating writing patterns into artwork can be a very worthwhile activity. Through practice your child will gradually learn to make all the strokes necessary to form letters. Once again, however, don't make her draw writing patterns without some other purpose attached. Encourage her to incorporate them into drawings, use them to make picture frames for drawings and other, similar uses.

Use patterns that are based on the way letters are formed:

*Spirals; circles; semicircles; zigzags; vertical, horizontal and slanted lines; arches and scallops.*

## Finger painting

Age: from around 3 on

### You will need

Liquid or powder paint. Water-soluble paste (the kind usually used to hang wallpaper works well). A clean shiny surface, such as a formica table or tray. Paper. Children and floor surfaces should be well protected!

### How to Play

Mix up the paint with the wallpaper paste until it is the consistency of thick soup. Put a few large spoonsful on to the shiny surface and ask your child to spread it around. Now she can practise writing with her fingers (among other things)! If she doesn't like what she's done, she can smooth over the design with her hand and start again. When the design is complete, take a large piece of paper and put it on the table over the design, so that it takes a print of the painting. At this stage you can either start again with another dollop of paint or clear up!

## Sewing

There are a number of different sewing activities your child can do to develop good hand-eye co-ordination.

ABOVE **You can use finger painting to create writing patterns – it's a lot more fun than even crayons and felt-tip pens, and you can create a picture of your efforts when you've finished!**

◆ Draw shapes such as circles and squares on a heavy piece of paper using a thick pen. With a small screwdriver puncture holes at intervals all round the perimeter of the shape. Show your child how to thread a thick tapestry needle with wool and how to put the needle and thread in and out of the holes. Once she's got the hang of this, show her how to fill in the holes right round the perimeter. Later draw the letters of your child's name in the same way and ask her to sew them. Make sure the lines follow the way in which the letter should be written (see the diagram on page 73). Put a cross where you want the sewing to begin. If you're worried about using needles and thread, start her off with shoe laces, which she can thread in and out of the holes.

◆ Buy cloth with holes already in it (Binca)

ABOVE **The more things you can think of to do with letter shapes – including sewing them – the more easily your child will learn them.**

and teach her how to make the different stitches. Always remember to go from simple stitches to those that are more difficult.

◆ Ask your child to draw a picture on some muslin. Put it into an embroidery frame and have her sew the picture.

## Dough or Clay

Playdough or clay is great fun to use and can also help dexterity. Like finger painting (and for much the same reasons!) it's probably best done on a formica table or on a tray.

◆ Roll out long sausages and form them into letters.

◆ Show your child how to roll spherical shapes and sausages. Make animals, houses, pots, whatever comes to mind.

# First steps towards reading and writing

Now that you have taken the first steps towards giving your child the foundation she needs to become a good reader and writer, there are some games you can play with her that will have a more direct impact on her acquisition of these skills. The activities covered in this chapter are those that you would find in any good Montessori classroom (or children's house, as Maria Montessori called it). We call them 'keys' to reading and writing. The word 'key' is very important: it is something that gives us access to things. When we want to make sense of a map we look up the key to help us make it more intelligible. A key doesn't give you the whole picture but it does provide you with some basic tools which help you to interpret the map more accurately. Making use of a key provides you with additional help if you want to make the best use of the map. A really helpful 'key' is one that provides you with just enough basic information to help you to find things out for yourself.

The following three activities – the Sound Game, the Sandpaper Letters and the Moveable Alphabet –build one upon the other. Don't be tempted to hurry them or skip forward to activities that may appear more familiar to you. They may appear to be very easy but don't underestimate their importance in the development of your child's ability to read and write. If she can master these three simple activities you will have created a very sound basis for literacy.

In playing these games you will accomplish the following:

◆ Raise your child's awareness of sounds and the way that words are made up of units of sounds.

◆ Help her recognize the symbols that represent those sounds.

◆ Help her begin to develop the correct hand movement for writing letters.

◆ Help her use symbols to write down her thoughts.

◆ Help her use her own writing as a bridge to reading.

## Raising your child's awareness of the sounds in her language

You will have already begun to read with your child, and many of the books you enjoy together will be story books which have rhyme and rhythm in them and some will be poetry and rhyme books. These will help her to recognize sound rhymes, which will be important later on when she begins to read since she will be able to predict many of the words she comes across because she knows they rhyme.

In addition to this natural way of listening to sounds and rhymes, you can play a variety of games to focus her attention on them and to raise her awareness of the role that sounds play,

## How the sound game inter-relates with the sandpaper letters and the moveable alphabet

| Level | | Age | |
|---|---|---|---|
| Level 1 | Initial sound, one object at a time no opportunity for mistakes | Age 2 ½ | |
| Level 2 | Initial sound, choice of two objects or more. Only one object can be identified as the correct answer | Age 2 ½–3 | |
| Level 3 | Initial sound, choice of part of room or whole room. Many objects can be identified with the same initial sound. | Age 3–3 ½ | Sandpaper Letters |
| Level 4 | Initial sound and last sound played at both Levels 2 or 3 as appropriate. | Age 3 ½– 4 ½ | |
| Level 5 | All the sounds in the word played at level 4, and then with any objects or any words. The object does not have to be 'spied'. | Age 3 ½ – 4 ½ | Moveable Alphabet |
| Level 6 | Take a sound and think of as many words as you can that contain the sound either at the beginning or end of the word or have the sound somewhere in between. | Age 4 ½– 6 | |

firstly in spoken language and then in reading and writing.

### The sound game

Age: from 2 ½ on

#### What you need to know

This game will help to make your child aware of the sounds that make up words. Play it as often as you can; it is one of the most important ways of preparing her for both writing and reading.

Make sure you say the sounds correctly! Your child will use the skills she develops in this game to help her 'sound out' the first words she writes and reads, so if you're careful with the sounds the rest is easy. They should be short, and you should try not to have much of a vowel sound to follow. For example 'b' should be sounded as in tub, not 'bu' as in 'bun'.

**Sound Chart**

| | | | | | | | |
|---|---|---|---|---|---|---|---|
| a | at | h | huh! | o | on | v | have |
| b | tub | i | in | p | tap | w | win |
| c | tack | j | fudge | q | quit | x | fox |
| d | mud | k | tack | r | rat | y | yes |
| e | egg | l | mill | s | fuss | z | buzz |
| f | off | m | hum | t | at | | |
| g | peg | n | hen | u | up | | |

Note that 'c' and 'k' sound the same.

If you can think of words where the consonants come mainly at the end of the word and the vowel sounds at the beginning, you will hear the sound you need to make.

Sadly, many alphabet books and friezes do not portray all the sounds accurately. Check through the books you have at home to make sure that the objects chosen to represent the

ABOVE **Level 1 of the Sound Game helps your child to connect sounds with familiar objects – here the sound 'b' with ball. Start with just one object at a time so that he won't get confused.**

sounds are correct. The sound that is most commonly misrepresented is 'x' which should sound as it does in 'fox' not as in xylophone which is pronounced 'z'!

The hard part for you will be listening to the sounds and forgetting (for the moment), how words are spelled. Don't panic! Children at this age have no idea that words can be spelled differently from the way they sound since they are not reading yet.

Since English in all its various dialects is a non-phonetic language, you will also need to practise sounds that are created when two single letters are combined; we call these digraphs.

### Common digraph sounds in English*

| ai | train play | ue | blue shoe zoom |
|---|---|---|---|
| ch | chip | er | her fir turn |
| ee | sleep leaf | oo | cook |
| th | path | ng | ring |
| ie | pie sky | ou | pout clown |
| th | with | or | for raw |
| oa | loaf window | sh | fish caption |
| ar | car | oy | boy spoil |

\* **Parents in the United States and Canada, and in Australia, New Zealand and South Africa will need to decide if there is a difference between the sounds 'or' and 'au'.**

Many other sound combinations will crop up as you start to explore language with your child, so be relaxed and use your own judgement as to how they should sound. What you are building in her is an awareness of the different sounds as they are heard in your own language or dialect.

### Let's practise!

Cover over the letters in each of the right-hand columns below and practise sounding the words in the left-hand column.

**Can you give the first sound of the following words?**

| | | | |
|---|---|---|---|
| cat | 'c' | bat | 'b' |
| chop | 'ch' | think | 'th' |
| knock | 'n' | centre | 's' |
| acorn | 'ai' | phone | 'f' |
| owl | 'ou' | australia | 'o' |

**Can you give the last sound of the following words?**

| | | | |
|---|---|---|---|
| mat | 't' | lamb | 'm' |
| dance | 's' | window | 'oa' |
| bench | 'ch' | cage | 'j' |
| tap | 'p' | party | 'ee' |
| cake | 'k' | books | 'x' |

**Can you give all the sounds in the following words?**

| | | | |
|---|---|---|---|
| dog | d-o-g | bottle | b-o-t-l |
| pamper | p-a-m-p-er | tough | t-u-f |
| house | h-ou-s | since | s-i-n-s |
| shoe | sh-ue | parrot | p-a-r-u-t |
| fetch | f-e-ch | quiet | qu-ie-e-t |

Once you've mastered the art of hearing and articulating the sounds of your language, you are ready to play the Sound Game, which is based on 'I spy with my little eye'. There are six levels to the game: level 1 can begin as early as two and a half and levels 5 and 6 should be played at around four and a half to five. Even if your child is older than two and a half when you start, you should still begin with level 1 and move her at her own pace through the different levels of the game.

## Level 1

Age: 2 ½ on

### What you will need

Gather together a few objects which your child can name and put them on a table in front of you. In the beginning avoid objects that start with similar sounds, such as 'p' and 'b', 'v' and 'w'.

### Purpose

To help your child to hear individual sounds at the beginning of words.

### How to Play

Choose one of the objects, for example a pen, and hold it out to show it to your child.

> 'I spy with my little eye something in my hand beginning with "p"'.

Your child will say 'pen'. Confirm that she is right. Yes, 'p' for 'pen'. Change the object and change the place where it can be found to keep the game interesting.

> 'I spy with my little eye something on the table beginning with "d"'......(perhaps doll)

> 'I spy with my little eye something I am touching beginning with 'c''.....(perhaps cup)

> 'I spy with my little eye something on my finger beginning with "r"'....(perhaps ring)

> 'I spy with my little eye something I am waving beginning with "h"'....(perhaps hand)

She will quickly grasp the rules of the game and happily tell you the names of the objects you are asking for. You will probably need to play this stage of the game for several weeks before she actually makes the connection between the sound that you say and the sound at the beginning of the object you have chosen. When she appears to be beginning to listen to the sounds, you can move on to Level 2.

## Level 2

Age: about 2½–3

### What you will need

Familiar objects you have gathered from around the house. In the beginning the initial sounds should be contrasting, but as the game proceeds over the weeks you can choose objects with similar initial sounds.

### Purpose

To help your child distinguish one initial sound from another.

### How to Play

Place two objects in front of you, each with different initial sounds (this could be, for instance, a car and a motorbike, as in the photograph, or cup and mug, and so on).

'I spy with my little eye something beginning with "m" '.

Your child now has to make a choice, and you will begin to hear how well she distinguishes sounds. Continue changing the objects but

only have two at any one time. To increase the challenge, place three objects in front of her and build gradually to having as many as five objects at once. You can now become much more subtle and show her objects beginning with similar sounds, for example, ring, watch and van.

## Level 3

Age: around 3½

### What you will need

Nothing! This level of the game can be played anywhere and at any time, and is closest to 'I spy'. This stage is a good one to play on car journeys. You will get tired of it before your child does.

### Purpose

To make your child aware that many objects may begin with the same sound. Once she has mastered this stage you are ready to introduce her to written letters. (See Sandpaper Letters on pages 69–70 of this chapter).

### How to Play

Choose an area of the room or garden, and a sound that represents more than one object in it. (If you run out of inspiration, use the photograph that illustrates this game!)

'I spy with my little eye some things over there by the window that begin with "b" '.

She will offer only one word, since this has been what has been expected thus far. You should volunteer some more and have her join in with you (basket, bottle, books, balls and so on). Now move on to another sound in the same or a different area.

LEFT **In Level 2 of the Sound Game, you can show him two *contrasting* sounds, for instance 'c' for car and 'm' for motorbike, and ask him which one is which.**

ABOVE **For Level 3 of the game, look for a variety of objects in the room that share the same sound – here you'll find 'b' is well represented in bird, basket, bottles, books and balls.**

Remember you are not asking her to search for one object that you are thinking of, but any item with that sound. As soon as enough items have been named, move on to another sound. You don't have to insist on your item being found. Move to other parts of the room or garden, then gradually move to the whole room or outdoors in general.

She can now take turns with you to choose the sound for the objects and, of course, you can begin to play 'I spy' in the more conventional way.

## Level 4

Age: around 3 ½–4 ½

### What you will need

At this stage you will need to return temporarily either to a collection of objects or to a part of the environment as in Level 3. What you do will depend on your

child and what help she needs for this stage. Regardless of whether you choose a collection of objects or part of the room, you will be looking for objects whose initial sounds are the same but whose last sounds are different. For example ball, bag, bracelet, or pen, peg, puppet. Choose enough objects to keep it interesting.

### Purpose

To help develop your child's awareness of sounds in words other than initial sounds. An awareness of all the sounds in words is essential when starting to write and read.

### How to Play

You say, 'I spy with my little eye, something on the table (or in part of the room) that begins with "b" and ends with "g" '. To begin with she may take a little time to learn to listen to the last sound. If she says 'ball', be positive in your response. 'Yes, ball does begin with "b" but I asked for something that begins with "b" and ends with "g"; let's listen to the last sound in

BELOW **It's important to help your child to listen for both first and last sounds in a word: in Level 4 of the Sound Game, you play with three objects, all beginning with the same letter but ending with different ones – bag, ball and bracelet.**

ball'. Say it slowly and carefully. Now help her to listen to the sounds of the other objects until she finds 'bag'.

Once she has mastered listening to the initial sounds and the last sounds for obvious objects, move to the whole environment and take it in turns to search for the objects, always giving the first and last sounds.

## Level 5

Age: 3 ½ – 4 ½

### What you will need
Nothing at all unless you wish to use objects.

### Purpose
To help your child to analyze all the sounds in a word. This is a skill that will be helpful when she is beginning to read and write. She will need to be at this level before using the Moveable Alphabet (see page 76 of this chapter).

### How to play
This stage should follow on naturally from the one before. Once your child can readily find a word that begins and ends with a particular sound, stop and listen for all the sounds in the word. Begin with fairly short words. For example if the word is 'cup' and she has identified that it begins with 'c' and ends in 'p' you could say, 'Let's listen to all the sounds in "cup". Let's say it slowly. C-u-p. Did you hear the sound after "c"? Let's say "cup" again'.

The two of you slowly say the word and identify each sound. C-u-p.

'Now we know all the sounds in "cup", let's find all the sounds in "pan", then "coffee" '. Gradually the words become longer and longer, and the two of you can have lots of fun finding more and more difficult words to sound out. You have stopped 'spying' the objects and can think of any words that you like.

## Level 6

Age: 4 ½ – 6

### What you will need
Nothing!

### Purpose
This stage is designed to use all the knowledge gathered thus far with regard to sounds, and to encourage your child to play with the sounds in words.

### How to Play
Think of a sound, for example 'm'. Now think of all the words that have the sound 'm' in them somewhere. Think of words with 'm' at the beginning: mat, munch, mother; 'm' at the end: farm, ham, drum; 'm' anywhere within them: marmalade, number, minimum etc. Have fun!

### Note
Remember to use the ages given above as a guide only and to progress at your child's pace. Some children will manage to listen to the sounds very easily and quickly while others will take longer; some will not need to progress in such a step by step way. You know your child and will be able to make the appropriate judgement.

## More games to help with sound recognition

### I spy rhyming words
This is a simple game where, instead of spying things that begin with a sound, you find things that rhyme with a word. For example, 'I spy with my little eye something that sounds like jug'. The answer may be 'mug' or 'rug'. Alternatively, 'I spy with my little eye something that rhymes with bee'. The answer could be 'me', 'tree', etc.

### Inventing poems
You can invent some funny 'nonsense' rhymes

with your child – this often appeals to her sense of humour.

High in a tree

I saw a ..... (your child says 'bee' or 'knee' or 'flea' or anything else that springs to mind)

Using all your powers of invention you now continue

| High in a tree | High in a tree |
| I saw a bee | I saw a flea |
| The bee saw me | It said tee hee |
| And flew on to my ..... | And then bit ..... |

### Sorting pictures that rhyme or begin with the same sounds

Once again a mail order catalogue can be very useful. Cut out different groups of objects that rhyme and that are familiar to your child. If you are good at drawing you could draw your own pictures of familiar objects. For example:

Jug, rug, mug

Bat, mat, hat, cat

Train, plane, chain

Pan, fan, van

Ask your child to sort the pictures according to the way they rhyme. On another day you could do the same for initial sounds. You could also mix them all up and play rhyming snap.

### Odd one out

Once you feel your child is able to judge which sounds rhyme, you can play this game using one group of pictures only and adding in a single picture that is the odd one out. Ask her to find the picture that doesn't rhyme. Alternatively, ask her to identify the picture that starts with a different sound to the others. For example:

ABOVE **Challenge your child to find the Odd Man Out in this collection! It's avocado in the first line (the others all begin with the letter 'c'), and grapes in the second (the others all begin with the sound 'p').**
LEFT **Sorting pictures that rhyme helps focus your child on the rhyme patterns in words. The objects used here were traced on to ordinary paper with a felt-tip pen in minutes. You can do the same thing with objects that begin with the same sound.**

Jug , rug, mug and bat

Book, bat, ball, boot and car

## Books

You can use any beautifully illustrated book to play 'I spy' – most of those recommended in Chapter 9 would be suitable. To make the game more interesting, try to find illustrations containing lots of detail and a variety of objects.

# The sandpaper letters

Once your child can play the Sound Game at level 3, she is ready to begin to identify the letters of the alphabet. It is important to wait until she has reached this stage; whenever we learn something new we build or graft it on to existing knowledge, so if your child is secure with the sounds she hears at the beginning of a word, she will find it easier to understand that the letter or symbol you wish to teach her is simply the way the sound that she already knows is written. In this way new learning becomes more straightforward as it rests on a firm foundation of previous experience.

You will need to make a set of letters for your child to learn, and from a substance that is tactile because you will teach her to feel the shape of the letter as well as to recognize it visually.

In using this approach, your child will have both a visual and

tactile experience of the letter, which means she will use more than one sensory channel to receive information and remember it. Often a child who struggles to remember the letter visually will remember it immediately when she is encouraged to feel it again.

In addition to receiving maximum sensory input to help her recognize letters, her hand is learning, well in advance of actually writing letters, how each letter is formed. You should make sure, therefore, that each letter can be felt in the way that it should be written. The more practice a child gets at feeling the letters, the more her hand will 'know' how to start and form a letter when writing it.

## Making the letters

Traditionally, these letters are made from the finest grade of sandpaper, which you should be able to find at your ironmonger or DIY centre. However, if you prefer you could also make them from velvet or even a coarse-quality paper. The important thing is for your child to be able to experience the tactile quality of the letter.

RIGHT **Feeling Sandpaper Letters is an easy way to familiarize your child with the shape of letters as they are written. Encourage her to feel around the shape while you say the sound 'f' or 's'. Understanding how letters are written will make it easier for her to recognize letters and words, and to write them.**

The letters should be large enough to enable her hand to get a really good feel of the shape of the letter. (There are templates in Chapter 9 of this book, which you could use to make the letters.)

You will need to mount the letters on board or thick card, and you should have three colours of card to distinguish between vowels, consonants and digraphs. Vowels, for instance, could be mounted on blue, consonants on pink and digraphs on green. The colour distinction will help your child to become aware of the difference between these types of letters. Choose colours that appeal to you but make sure that you continue to use these colours for the other letter games in the book too!

If you know that your child is right- or left-handed, the letter can be placed more to the right (for a right-hander) and more to the left (for a left-hander). This creates a wider space on the card for the child to hold it steady with one hand while she traces over the letter with the other. If you are unsure whether she is right- or left-handed you will be safer placing the letter centrally on the card.

## Make the following letters:

### vowels
(blue background): a e i o u (y)

### consonants
(pink background): b c d f g h j k l m n p (q) r s t v w x (y) z

In some languages 'y' is a vowel, and in languages where 'q' is always followed by 'u', make a digraph instead of a single letter.

In non-phonetic languages (languages where there are more sounds than letters to represent them), children will require additional help. English is non-phonetic and, depending on the country in which it is being spoken, there are approximately 40-45 different sounds. Identifying these sounds, or digraphs, can be very helpful, although unfortunately they can often be spelled in several ways – for example the sound 'ai' as in train, can also be spelled 'cake' or 'reign' or 'play'. Choose the spelling that seems most common or appropriate for your child's early reading when you create your digraph letters, or follow the suggestions given above. (See Chapter 3 if you want to check the sounds they make.)

### Digraphs
(green background): qu ai ee ie oa ue ar er or ch sh th oy ou oo

(In North America and Australia, New Zealand and South Africa an additional digraph 'au' may be useful. The sound would be represented by the word 'awful' while the 'or' sound would be represented by 'fork'.)

### Note
It is important to give your child only what is essential to get her writing and reading; if you try to give her every possible digraph that exists the task will be overwhelming and instead of helping her you will slow her down and even hinder her progress.

There is currently much debate as to what kind of letter shapes children should learn. In the past it was felt to be important to teach a child to recognize and write printed letters in the first instance, then when she was older to teach her to write with a more cursive or 'joined up' hand. However, research has now shown us that children can learn to read very well, even if they do learn with a more cursive style of letter, since they are used to seeing print of all types around them and have no difficulty in translating one style of letter to another. Equally, new research shows that it is just as easy for a child to learn a more 'flowing' style of handwriting as it is to learn the 'ball and stick' principles of print, and in the end she does not need to learn everything twice. Indeed, children often will not form printed letters as they should be written because rather than seeing 'a' as a continuous line they see a circle and a stick (hence the description ball and stick), and will form the letter accordingly. This can be very difficult to undo at a later stage when teaching the correct formation of letters.

Try to avoid teaching your child to write in capital letters as her first experience. Usually capitals present no problems for children as there are many ways of writing them correctly. They can easily learn these after they have mastered lowercase letters.

It is lowercase letters that require careful learning. They will determine the ease with which children will form a good flowing hand later on, so it is worthwhile to begin at the right moment, offering Sandpaper or velvet Letters that will prepare the eye and the hand for both writing and reading.

## Teaching your child Sandpaper Letters

Age: about 3–3 ½ (when your child can do level 3 of the Sound Game and while she is intensely interested in touching things). If your child has very poor hand/eye co-ordination continue to practise the activities in Chapter 3. It is important that she does not find feeling the letters too difficult.

Teach only three letters at any one time and mix vowels, consonants and digraphs together. For each lesson choose letters that sound different and look different. (In addition you may wish to look at Chapter 5 to choose letters that come from the same writing group.)

Choose a moment when your child is ready to sit down for a while, and never force her to learn the letters. Don't be disappointed if she is unable to say them at the end of the first time you play the game. Be positive and use praise at all times. Some children need to play the game a number of times before they begin to show you that they remember the letters you are teaching them.

If your child seems unable to remember the letters at the end of the first lesson don't be negative in any way. Don't go back to the beginning of the lesson and try to repeat the whole thing again or she will swiftly feel some sort of compulsion to 'get it right'. Don't go back to the same letters the next day either, simply choose three different letters. You must not risk giving your child a sense of failure just as you are about to embark on one of the most rewarding activities of her life. Having successfully helped her to achieve so much in such a short space of time, don't risk turning her off because of your own expectations. So if she seems to be uninterested you must stop and wait until she is!

During the lesson encourage your child to feel the letters as often as possible but make sure she is feeling them correctly. If you can manage to find 10 minutes a day to play this game she will soon be confident about recognizing the letters. Try to play the game when she requests it – she will progress much faster if she has chosen to do the activity herself. It can help to remind her that when she is ready to play the letter game she just has to tell you.

### How to feel the letters

Feel each letter using the index and middle fingers of your dominant hand. If your child is left-handed, you should feel them with your left hand. Feel them in the way that they are written (see the diagram opposite). Make a point where you start and complete the action in one smooth movement. It may also be useful to add a line at the base of the card so that your child knows which way up to feel it.

### How to Play

To play this game you will need to use the

three-period lesson described in Chapter 2, adapting it as outlined below to teach the letters. Make sure you are sitting beside your child and not opposite her – she must always be able to see the letters the right way up.

**Stage 1**: Choose three letters. You may want to choose them from the same writing family (see Chapter 5) – for example: 'c' 'd' and 'a'. Begin by playing the Sound Game, asking your child to spy anything beginning with 'c'. (Cat, cup, card etc.) You can join in to help. Now show her the letter 'c'.

This is how we write 'c'. Feel the letter and say the sound of the letter (not the name) and help your child to do the same. Feel it, using the index and middle fingers of your writing hand (use the hand she will write with; these will be the fingers she will use to guide a pencil later

BELOW **It is important to feel each Sandpaper Letter in the way it is written. The dot marks the place to start, then your child should follow the direction indicated by the arrows.**

on). So have your left hand hold the letter steady and trace over the surface in one smooth, flowing movement with your right hand if she is right-handed and do the reverse if she is left-handed.

Do the same for each of the other letters.

Stage 2: This stage is the longest one because your child needs time and plenty of repetition in order to associate the sound and letter shape together. Be patient. Each one of us requires a different amount of practice time whenever we learn anything new. Your child is unique and you need to sense how long she needs to feel confident of recognizing the letter you are asking for.

Ask at random for the letters, using their sounds. Ask in many ways but keep the instructions short and simple. Each time the letter is identified correctly, encourage her to feel it and repeat the sound. You will need to do this too. Always return the identified letter to the group once it has been felt, and continue with your requests. Mix the letters up each time to add excitement to the game and to help her to really look for the letter you are asking for. If she does not want to feel the letters you should do so anyway. Be inventive and have fun! Some examples:

Touch 'm'

Find 'o'

Put 't' over here

Feel 'o'

Where's 'm'

Hold 't'

Be careful not to follow the same order each time, to look at the letter you want or request the last letter you touched. Children are very quick to work out patterns and systems!

ABOVE **Once she's got the hang of letter shapes and sounds, you can move on. Ask her to match the sounds (and letters) to familiar objects in the house; she may bring you several things beginning with 'm' in addition to mug!**

Stage 3: Point to one of the letters and ask your child if she remembers which one it is. If she can remember, encourage her to feel it once more. If she can't, encourage her to feel it and see if this jogs her memory. If she does not remember, say it for her and don't dwell on the fact that she couldn't tell you what it said. Focus on the letters that she can remember and make her feel pleased she can remember them.

If she gets muddled, don't worry. Perhaps you didn't spend enough time establishing the sound and shape in the first stage; perhaps she lost interest. Whatever the reason, she has at least three years to make this connection, so you must not see it as a disaster. Feel the letters and give her the names again, then happily bring the lesson to a close. Come back to it another day.

### Reinforce what your child knows

Each day, before teaching your child any new letters, always go over the ones she knows already so that she can see the fruits of her efforts. This can be very encouraging for her and by identifying the letters she knows you are encouraging her to learn a few more. If she is unsure of any letters previously learned, include them once again in the next lesson but still keep to a maximum of three letters at a time.

## More games to play to help with letter recognition

You can play many games with the Sandpaper Letters as they grow in number, which will help to encourage her even more. As the number of recognized letters increases you can encourage her to count the number she knows. She can tip-toe back and forth between rooms collecting and feeling the letters you ask for. Encourage her to feel around the edge of any letters she sees on posters, T-shirts and magazines.

### Letters and objects

Have a basket or bag of objects that begin with the sounds of the letters she knows and a set of Sandpaper Letters corresponding with these sounds. See if she can match the object with the correct letter.

Ask your child to collect objects from around the room that have the same sounds as the letters she knows. Again have a set of these letters handy. Encourage her to put the object next to the correct letter card. Whenever possible encourage her to feel the letter in the way that it should be written.

Choose only one letter and ask her to collect as many objects as possible that begin with that sound.

Remember that you will be continuing to play the Sound Game while you are introducing the Sandpaper Letters, and if you are still on level 3 you could ask her to spy objects beginning with the sounds of the letters she recognizes. This would mean holding up the letter card rather than saying the sound out loud. Perhaps your child could choose a letter and ask you the question!

### Letters and actions

Hide some of the letter cards in the room and ask her to find each one. 'Can you find "t" '?

Place the letter cards around the room and ask her to hop to 'm', jump to 'l', tiptoe to 'oy' and so on.

### Letters and books

When you are reading books to your child, point out some of the letters she knows. Perhaps, if she is

LEFT **Making an Alphabet Book is easy. The letter 'c' is going to be illustrated by sticking down a picture of a crown and a cat, both cut out of a magazine. The letters in this case have been written by an adult.**

interested, you can encourage her look at the pages of the book to see if she can recognize any of the letters herself.

### Making an alphabet and other books

Write one of the letters your child knows on a piece of paper and look through pictures and magazines with her. Cut out those objects that start with that letter. (A mail order catalogue can be very useful for this.) If she isn't able to cut out the picture herself then you do it, but let her stick it on to a backing paper to make a 'page'. If she is able to, you could encourage her to draw her own pictures of objects she can think of that begin with the letter. Encourage her gradually to build up her own alphabet book. Tie it together when it is finished so that it looks really nice – see Chapter 9 for some simple suggestions for this.

Make a zigzag book and write a letter at the top of each section. Then ask your child to try to find (and stick down under the letter) pictures of objects that start with the letter. Another version of this would be to write a word across the top of each section and stick in pictures of objects that start with each of the letters of each word.

### The jolly postman

Make an envelope for each letter of the alphabet and use each one to collect pictures that begin with that sound.

### Jigsaw puzzles

There are many different jigsaw puzzles available that have objects and lower-case letters attached. Before you buy them make sure that the objects in the pictures reflect the sound of the letter accurately. As your child gets better and better at fitting the shape of the piece into its socket you can begin to find out how many she recognizes.

### Alphabet twister

Do you remember the game 'Twister'? At the spin of an arrow you placed your feet on a coloured circle on a playing mat until one player could no longer stand up. This is the same game, only this time you need to write some of the letters your child knows on a paper circle on a mat in washable ink. Play the game in the same way, spinning the arrow, but this time call out the sound of the letter that the foot must land on. Write each letter at least once on each half of the circle. You can play with just three letters or as many as your child knows.

### Jigsaw mat

Sponge mats put together like jigsaw puzzles are lots of fun to build and play on, and many of them have the letters of the alphabet as separate insets. Putting the whole mat together can be great fun on its own but you can also invent lots of games to play on it. Your child could match objects to the different letters or jump from one letter to another; or she could see if she could touch all the letters of her name in one go with all the parts of her body. The rest I leave up to you!

You will find that within a very short period of time your child will be able to recognize many of the letters of the alphabet by playing just two simple games: the Sound Game and the Sandpaper Letters. You will have prepared her well for writing and reading.

## The moveable alphabet – the bridge to reading and writing

Once your child is familiar with about three quarters of the Sandpaper Letters you can begin to encourage her to write down words, sentences and poems with a set of letters you have made for this purpose. We call it the Moveable Alphabet. This game provides the vital link for your child between reading and writing.

Your child must experience for herself the power of using symbols to leave messages, stories and poems for others to read. The act of writing something down gives permanence and therefore importance to what may otherwise be spoken and forgotten.

Giving her letters that have already been prepared divorces the creative and expressive side of writing from the slower and more underdeveloped skill of writing by hand. The development of both of these areas will progress along parallel lines for a while: in this way the actual act of handwriting, which needs practice and repetition, doesn't hold up her growing ability to use language in its written form to express thought.

The two parallel paths are:

◆ Expressive and creative writing, which is a vital foundation for reading and writing (for which we use the Moveable Alphabet).

◆ Preparing the hand to write letters fluently and easily (for which we use the Sandpaper Letters: see Chapter 5).

These paths will join together quite naturally later on. You will find that your child will spontaneously begin to label drawings and write messages, and eventually, as writing becomes a natural physical skill, the alphabet that you used to allow for the flowering of her creative writing will not need to be used.

In addition to the other benefits

that accrue to your child from being able to write expressively, as she begins to write using the Moveable Alphabet letters she will directly experience the way in which letters make words, and how print goes from left to right and from top to bottom. It will give her an opportunity to connect writing directly with speech and, in finding out how easy it is to make words by analyzing sounds, she will be very quick to make the leap between writing things down and actually being able to read back what she has written.

Don't make your child read back any of her written work with the Moveable Alphabet. Trust in all the preparation you have done and in her. To begin with she will remember what she has written and 'feel' that she is reading, and this is a big boost to her confidence: a child who feels she is a reader can become a reader. But one day as she is composing her stories you will notice

LEFT **The Moveable Alphabet can be invaluable in helping your child recognize letters. Get him used to it by encouraging him to take out and put back individual letters into their compartments.**

that her attention to each word differs as she 'reads' what has been put down. Words that can be easily remembered are being studied and pronounced more slowly. Some words will be recognized as 'sight' words, some worked out. She has taken the magic step all by herself and now you have both an author and a reader.

### What your child needs to know before using the moveable alphabet

**The Sound Game:** She must be able to break words down into their different sounds. Remember that doesn't mean as they are spelled but as they sound. This is around level 5 of the Sound Game.

**The Sandpaper Letters:** She should know three-quarters of the letters, including some digraphs and certainly all the vowels. Working with the Moveable Alphabet encourages her to learn the remaining letters as she discovers that she needs them to write down the words she is thinking of.

### What you need to know

This activity is fun. You supply the letters your child needs if she doesn't know them. Spelling doesn't matter at this stage – you will help your child to spell using other games that will appear later in the book. Gradually, as your child plays the other parallel games (Puzzle Words and Key Sound Envelopes, Chapters 6 and 7) the words that she 'sounds out' in the beginning will start to be spelled more accurately. This activity is collaborative in the beginning, so if your child wishes a permanent record of what she has written you will have to write it down for her. However, you must make sure you write it down using the correct spelling.

### How to make the moveable alphabet

Use the same shape of letter you used for the Sandpaper Letters only slightly smaller (use the templates in Chapter 9 and reduce them on a photocopier). Cut out 10-15 copies of each letter. Use one colour for consonants and one colour for vowels. (It helps if they are the same colour that you chose for the Sandpaper Letters.) Remember to cut out appropriate-coloured dots for the 'j' and the 'i'. Place the letters in the compartments of a large box (it needs to have 26 separate ones for the letters and an extra one for the dots). If possible try to have compartments large enough to take each letter flat and glue one on to the bottom of each one so that it is easy to replace the letters in their correct compartment. Make the letters a reasonable size – if they are too small they become too fiddly and your child will get frustrated trying to use them.

### Before you play the game

Bring out the box and play a game to help her find where each letter is. 'Can you find "m"'? 'Let's see if you know this one'? (This is a good indicator of how many letters she knows and may encourage her to set about learning the ones she doesn't). Take some letters out of the box, mix them up and ask her to find their 'homes'. While you are busy doing other things have her fetch different letters from the box for you. The further away you are the more fun it is. Let her ask you to do the same thing. Take a letter and see if you can find it in her favourite book. Link the letters in the box to the letters in the book. While you are familiarizing yourself and her with the letters, point out which way up the letters go and show her that the 'i' and 'j' have a dot added to the top.

### Playing the game

The writing down of words should stem from a spontaneous conversation with your child and should be done for a reason: all writing is purposeful. Perhaps you might decide to write down the names of all her favourite toys, foods, people; you may wish to write a menu for

lunch or supper; or perhaps you want to leave a message for a relative or remind yourself that the oven is on. Decide to write your child a message which you will then read and she can write her answer. A simple 'yes' or 'no' may be sufficient in the beginning. Have your digraphs nearby, as you will probably need them.

Your message may go something like this.

'Let's go shopping – you can help me write a list. What do you think we need? I know, eggs. Can you tell me the sounds in "eggs" '?

Your child should be able to sound out eggs. She may sound it e-g-s or e-g-z – it doesn't matter! Ask her for the first sound again:

*Adult* 'What did it start with'?

*Child* 'e'

*Adult* 'Can you find "e" '?

Your child finds it and places it on the table or floor, wherever you are. Move it to the left and just under the box.

> *Adult* 'What sound comes next'?
>
> *Child* 'e-g – "g" '
>
> *Adult* 'Can you find it'?

Show your child how to place it next to the first letter. Be careful not to ask for the second sound or the third sound; she will not have a concept of there being a certain number of letters in a word. By asking for the 'next' sound you can explain that the 'next' sound must go 'next' to the other letter.

Should your child produce a 'z' for the last sound accept it and carry on. You should not be concerned with spelling at this stage.

> *Adult* 'Look, you've written "eggs". Let's write another word on our list'.

Choose another word or let your child choose one. Very soon you'll have a terrific list of words that you have written together. Throughout the game encourage her to take the lead as much as possible, and try to choose shorter words to start with, and if possible those that are mostly phonetic for the first few. If she cannot find a particular letter-sound correspondence simply give her the letter. This process should be smooth and effortless and a real delight to your child who is truly able to write and express thoughts with very little effort.

### Dealing with sounds such as 'ch' 'oy' etc.

When these crop up produce the Sandpaper digraph and have your child identify the two letters that make this up. Prior to this she learned these as 'one picture' but as we are now analyzing the sounds in words she should be able to identify that two letters go together to make a single sound. Keep them handy so that she can easily refer to them.

Don't worry about spelling at this stage. The important thing for your child to feel is that she is able to write easily and fluently and that her message is understood. Now you can encourage her to use the alphabet every day. You can write down poems and nursery rhymes which you both know and gradually little stories – sometimes a good story can last three sentences and sometimes they are much longer. Don't worry about capital letters at this stage. Keep everything very simple and just watch your child become a 'writer'!

LEFT **Kum to mi party!** Once she understands the principle of creating words from the Moveable Alphabet letters, your child can have lots of fun writing messages for her friends.

Very quickly, as your child becomes more practised in her use of the Moveable Alphabet, she will become aware of a number of important things. By taking out the letters and putting them together she becomes aware of how words are formed and made. She also understands that she should place them from left to right, that there should be a gap between each new word and that the gap is usually about the space of one letter. Don't be tempted to use objects with the Moveable Alphabet – you will hinder the creative development of her writing and limit it to a very mechanical level.

Give her lots of encouragement. If she wishes, she could illustrate what she has 'written'. Don't encourage her to copy what she has written just yet, it's too soon for the hand to write accurately and at speed. Of course, if she spontaneously begins to write you messages then be very encouraging and supportive, but try not to suggest that she copies what she has written with the Moveable Alphabet as this will make a chore out of something that is a pleasure. When she can write easily and well, she will not want to use the Alphabet any more and her ability to write well and creatively will quite naturally make it obsolete.

You will be surprised at the variety and quality of what your child may write with the Moveable Alphabet over a period of time. This poem was written by a child in a Montessori school when he was four and a half, using the Moveable Alphabet.

Autum iz cool and culrful

Thai raik leavz

And maik bomfierz.

This is a wonderfully creative poem for a child of this age to have written. I have long since lost contact with him, but the beauty of his poem remains permanently with me. He could not have physically written down the letters for this poem – it would have taken too long and been too laborious for him. He could have asked one of his teachers to be his scribe, but I suspect that in order to write this poem he needed to be alone, quietly thinking of what autumn meant to him and how he would like to describe it. I hope I need not add that this poem was not the product of his teacher suggesting that the children might all like to write a poem about Autumn! He chose to write it himself.

## Please remember not to ask your child to read what she has written

If we return to our vision of the two processes of reading and writing you will remember that writing is very close to speech and in the beginning simply requires that we analyze sounds. Reading has to make use of a number of additional strategies. You will find that when your child writes with the Moveable Alphabet she will need you to read back what has been written in the beginning. Sometimes she will 'chant' the words she has written because she can remember them. Be delighted with her.

One day however, she will begin to study the words she has written and will start to read them back to you spontaneously. Usually you can easily tell the difference between the moment of remembering and the moment of reading, as she seems to spend longer actually looking at the letters and linking them together into a word, and her attention seems different when she is reading.

This is a magical moment and can happen as quickly as a few days after the first introduction to the Alphabet, although sometimes it takes longer. The important thing for you and your child is that it happens spontaneously; she should simply find herself able to do it.

Suddenly your child not only feels herself to be a reader, she is a reader! Her eyes will linger on words that you have just read; her attention will be caught by a single word. Silently you will see her lips moving as she confirms her knowledge of how that particular word sounds. You will also notice her becoming more confident in recognizing 'whole' words that she has seen frequently in books or when she is out and about with you.

When your child has reached the stage described above she will be keen to progress her reading skills; this would be a good time to begin to play the games in Chapter 6 with her.

## Games to play that involve writing messages

### Magnetic letters on the fridge

You may have to buy more than one set of magnetic letters to get enough vowels to make this work well. Write simple messages to your child and encourage her to write back.

### Sponge letters in the bath

These letters are fun as they stick to the side of the bath. Your child can write answers to questions such as, 'Have your cleaned your teeth'? 'Where's your blue bucket'?

### Magnetic pictures with words

Well chosen puzzles with words, such as those by Jolly Learning, are cleverly done as the letters can go in any order and your child will have to sound them out to get the word right.

### Printing sets and stencils with letters

Simple printing sets and stencils can help children to print their own letters and write their own labels and messages.

### Junior Boggle

This is an excellent game to encourage children to form words. The cards that come with the game have a huge number of phonetic words in addition to others that you can use as your child becomes more proficient at spelling. In addition, because the words are written clearly on each card, she is able to correct herself if she doesn't quite manage to get it right.

## Computers

Don't be in a hurry to introduce your child to the computer. Unless you can find a keyboard with lower-case letters on it, wait a little bit longer. Most children have an uncanny way of 'knowing' many of the upper-case letters and once your child seems to recognize them easily, a simple lesson in how to write messages using a computer can be useful. Beware however, because computers also need a lightness of touch and a knowledge of how to create spaces, and you do not wish to extend the time your child spends in front of the screen. Children, as a general rule, find that writing by hand is much quicker than writing on screen to begin with and this should be encouraged. An error on the computer can be quickly corrected; the hand, however, needs to develop to a stage where accurate writing is not a chore.

ABOVE **Encourage your child to write messages to you and, as she begins to read, leave messages for her around the house. We can only guess what treat awaits in the refrigerator!**

## Acting as a scribe

Encourage your child to send messages to other people:

◆ A thank-you card for presents received.

◆ A 'hello, how are you' message.

◆ A birthday greeting.

◆ A story about what she has done that day.

Ask her to dictate to you what she would like you to write for her. Write down exactly what she says then read it back to her so that she can

ABOVE Letter stencils can be employed in lots of ways and are simple to use. Labels for a book or clothes shelf, or names to go with a set of Classified Cards are only two possibilities.

decide if she agrees with what is written. Perhaps she would like to include a picture or some 'writing'. Encourage her to decorate the paper that you have written on so that the note is truly a collaborative venture between the two of you.

As you play these games, watch the way in which your child, although speaking, seems aware that she has become a writer. She will search for the right words to use and as she becomes aware of the link between stories and her own dictated story, she will begin to use story convention. Many will begin with 'One day...' or even 'Once upon a time...' and the words 'the end' can come very suddenly! Similarly, as she uses the Moveable Alphabet to compose stories you will observe the way in which her language changes to a more authorial style rather than conversational. Because you have read to her so often you have given her a lot of experience and

knowledge about books and how they work. She quite naturally assumes the role of author and an important step towards literacy has been achieved

## Your child's own writing

When your child begins to write with ease (see Chapter 5) you can encourage her to play all the above games by writing them herself. And leaving her 'fun' messages should encourage her to leave you fun messages too.

An examples received from one of my own children is:' I hav left'.

A message sent from the six-year-old to the four-year-old went as follows:

'Will the person in the bottom bunk bed please not disturb me when he wakes up in the morning, Tom.'

Well, the four-year-old woke up early and realized that the 'note' must be for him. He came to my bedroom and woke me up at 6.30 a.m. to ask me to read it to him − I must admit I felt like adding my name to the bottom of the note as well! The act of writing the note was helpful and beneficial to both children, though. The four-year-old was able to learn more about the nature of the printed word and immediately recognized, even though he couldn't read it, that the note was meant for him. The six-year-old felt happy and confident that he had expressed and conveyed his feelings in a non-verbal way, and that the message had been received and noted!

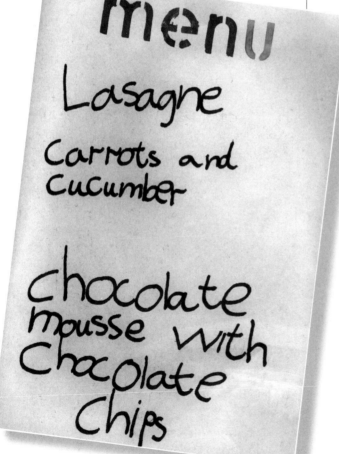

# CHAPTER FIVE

# Learning to write the letters

Having begun to teach your child to recognize the letters of the alphabet, you can now also start to help her write them. In addition to all the general preparations you've been making to create a 'readiness' to write, you should now also concentrate on some specific skills: handwriting is an art that has to be learned. As with any skill, if you begin by forming bad habits correcting them can take a lot of time and effort, but with the right help at the beginning, you will be able to help her acquire good handwriting habits and skills which will stay with her all her life.

Here are some points to bear in mind before you start.

## Posture

Make sure she is sitting comfortably at a table – it's helpful if her feet can reach the floor. The height of the table and the chair should allow her arms and hands to be at a good angle to the tabletop so that her arms are free to move across the paper without being cramped or tense. You should also check that she is not sitting too close to the table or too far away. If she is left-handed you may need to seat her slightly higher so that she can see the marks she is making over the top of her hand.

## Space

Make sure there is plenty of space on the table so that pencils or crayons can be placed within reach, but not in the way of either the paper or her arm. Don't sit too close to her as this may cause her to swivel or turn her body into an awkward position.

## Writing tools

Provide a variety of pens or pencils. These should vary in colour, allowing her to exercise aesthetic choice. Children seem to develop strong preferences for colours at a very early age and favourites are pink, purple, red, blue and green! Provide ordinary lead pencils and also some felt-tip pens. The thickness of the writing implements should also vary as some children find it easier to grip a slightly thicker pencil while others may prefer those that are triangular or hexagonal in shape. You will need to observe which pencils your child seems to prefer and which she feels most comfortable holding. The points of the pencils should be sharp but not brittle.

## Storing pens and pencils

Have a container of some kind for the pencils and pens – a jar or beaker will serve very well, as they can be taken out and put back easily. Pencil cases can be fun to use a little later on, but at this stage the pencils tend to be left out and get in the way or drop off the table, all of which will interfere with your child's ability to focus her attention on the task.

Don't be tempted to cram too many pens and pencils into one container as this will not help her to make a choice. If you really want to observe which pencil or pen works well for her, she needs to be able to see what's on offer. If there are too many pens to choose from she will find it impossible to know which choices she has and will settle for whatever catches her immediate attention.

Try to keep this container and the paper that you have selected in a place accessible to your child. She can then choose when she wishes to 'write' by herself, in addition to the times that you choose to write together.

## Paper

Whether you choose to start writing on paper or on a blackboard, try to ensure that whatever you select is of good quality – there is nothing more frustrating than flimsy paper or a shiny blackboard. To encourage a good hand, the surface being used should not be slippery, nor should your child be forced to press hard on it to make a mark. Don't fix the paper in any way as she will need to swivel it to suit the hand she is writing with. A firm table mat can serve as a good surface to put under paper, or a plastic floor tile if you have one large enough; failing this a large piece of blotting paper or heavy-grade painting paper may do.

You may need to help her place the paper in an appropriate position. Usually right-handed children need the paper slightly to the right of their body in front of their right hand, while left-handed children need the paper slightly to the left in front of their left hand. Some children like to angle the paper: a right-hander may angle the top slightly to the left and a left-hander may angle it either slightly to the left or slightly to the right. Try not to have paper that is too large

ABOVE **A bad position will make writing much more difficult, and could give your child bad habits from the start. This little girl is making the best of a bad job: her arm is not free to move across the writing surface and her back does not have the appropriate support.**

RIGHT **The same girl is now in a perfect position for writing at her child-size table: her arm is free and at the right height for the table, and her legs are stable. If buying her a table of her own is impossible, then raise her on telephone directories or buy a tall stool so that she can write more easily.**

to manipulate – A5 size will be about right to begin with.

### Decorating the undermat

If you decide to use a table mat or heavy-grade paper under the paper your child will write on, you could encourage her to decorate it to provide markers so that she'll know where to position her writing paper. Once she has found an optimum angle for her paper, ask her to put a little star at each corner on the undermat or paper, to mark her position.

## Pencil hold

Check that your child is holding the pen or pencil appropriately. There are a number of acceptable holds: a good one will usually involve her holding the pencil between her thumb and index finger with the middle finger acting as a support. The blunt end of the pencil can be relatively upright or slant along the line of the child's forearm. Any tension in the grip of the hand will not help her to write and may indicate that she is not holding the pencil in the best position. The important thing to remember is that there are several ways she can hold it – most of us were taught that there was only one way and we either conformed to it or were told that we held it 'incorrectly'. Your child may discover a hold that works but has not tradition-ally been acceptable. For example, a comfortable one may involve the shaft of the pencil resting between the first and second fingers rather than between the first finger and thumb.

## Light

Last of all make sure that your child can see what she is writing. Is there enough light falling

ABOVE **A good pen hold is just as important as a good writing pose; here the hand is relaxed, with the fingers comfortably controlling the pencil. Note the angle of the hand in spite of the fact that the child is left-handed.**

ABOVE LEFT **This pen hold is much less comfortable than the other two: the child's hand and shoulder are tense, and the thumb in control will soon cramp his hand.**

LEFT **This is a less orthodox hold than the one above right, but it's just as good. Whether you are left- or right-handed it would enable you to exercise good control.**

on the paper? Does her hand create a shadow over her writing?

Having prepared yourself as carefully as possible you can now start to help her to develop good handwriting techniques.

## Right- or left-handed?

It's not always easy to tell if your child is right-handed or left-handed when she is very young. Be relaxed about whichever hand your child uses to draw or write with. Some children use both hands for a variety of tasks. You might like to ask your child to use whichever hand she feels will make the best job of writing the letters. If she appears to be favouring her left hand, then here are some tips to make life a little easier for her.

◆ Sit her slightly higher on her chair so that her left arm is able to travel freely across the paper. A telephone directory can give the necessary stability; cushions could make her feel insecure.

◆ If possible arrange things so that both of her feet are on the ground.

◆ Place the paper slightly to the left of the mid-line of her body. The slanting of the paper should be left to the child, but try to make sure she has a relaxed and comfortable body position.

◆ Encourage her to use a writing implement that flows smoothly over the page, such as a felt-tip pen.

◆ Make sure that she has enough space to place her paper to the left.

◆ Check that she is able to see what she has written – sometimes the thumb obscures it. Suggest that she holds the pencil a little higher up the shaft, further from the point of the pencil if she seems to be having problems seeing it.

## Forming the letters

When children write a letter it is important to remember that this is largely to do with developing, from the beginning, the habit of forming the letters in the right way. Your child can learn to do this easily once she has relatively good control of her hands. Letter writing is learned and, just like learning to walk, once you can do it, it just comes naturally. It's very important for her to get off to a good start and the following activities will help her hand to develop naturally the kind of movement required to write the letters. The more practice she has the easier it will be. Remember that it is much more difficult to undo bad habits than to learn good ones from the beginning! You will need to make sure that she starts starts a letter in the correct place and is able to write it following the correct flow of the letter. (See the Sandpaper Letters diagram on page 73)

## Choosing a script

There are many differing opinions about what kind of letters to use. It is not advisable to teach your child to write using capital letters – she will learn these fairly easily at a later stage. Your first concern will be to teach her to write using lower-case letters and you must decide on the style of these from the start. The two main styles are print, and cursive (see templates, page 142).

I would recommend that you teach your child some form of cursive script from the very beginning for the following reasons.

◆ *Cursive script 'flows' and it is easy for your child's hand to move across it smoothly.* Print tends to be more abrupt in movement and print letters often lead children to look at the letters and write them using what is called the ball and stick formula. This will frequently lead to letters being formed incorrectly and bad habits can quickly become established.

◆ *The shapes of cursive letters are less likely to make letters look like mirror images of themselves, as you can see below.*

b d,  p q
bd   pq

◆ *Learning cursive letters means that, when your child gets older, she will be able to join them up very easily.* She will therefore only need to learn how to form letters once. Letters that aren't formed properly become a hazard when she gets to the stage of joining them up. You shouldn't expect her to join her letters until she can easily achieve the correct 'movement' for each letter (that is, starting the letter in the right place and moving her hand in the right direction to complete the letter).

◆ *When you are first teaching your child individual letters, it is helpful to create exit strokes on them which will allow her the possibility of joining one letter to another in the future.* This is another reason for preferring cursive script. When forming a print letter children will tend to exert most pressure on the pencil when finishing the letter on the baseline; joined up writing actually requires the hand to do the opposite. When joining letters together the hand needs less pressure as it moves from the finishing point of one letter to the starting point of the next. Although most parents will not need to be concerned about teaching their child joined up writing, it is as well to prepare her hand now, rather than create a habit that will need to be altered in the future. Be wary, however, of letter styles that have too many loops. The writing styles they produce may look beautiful but often only work if there is plenty of time to write and no pressure.

◆ *Cursive script is faster to write.* If handwriting is to serve the purpose for which it is intended, it must be something that can be done, ultimately, at speed, without disintegrating into illegibility or creating a hand that feels cramped or tired.

Finally, it is up to you. If you are unconvinced by the arguments above, I would suggest that you try to discover what type of script your child will use when she begins formal schooling, and choose that model for your Sandpaper Letters.

The following games are fun to play and will make sure that your child's hand is moving in the right direction in preparation for using a pencil. You can start playing them when she is able to recognize and feel many of the Sandpaper Letters well. You'll need to play all of these games at a table, or on the floor.

## Sorting into families
Age: around 3 ½–4
### You will need
A set of Sandpaper Letters
### Purpose
This game will help your child to explore which letters belong together because of the way they are written. Although it would appear that most letters have their own individual shape, there are distinct family groups and getting to know them will act as a key to her understanding. Instead of there being 26 individual letters, each of which is a distinct and separate shape, she will come to understand that mastering the shape of one letter gives you knowledge of how to write others.
### How to play
Separate out all the Sandpaper Letters your child knows, other than digraphs, and suggest that you sort them into families. It's probably best to do one 'family' at a time to begin with until the sorting process becomes easier.

Take the letter 'c' and ask your child to feel it and say the sound 'c'. You might suggest that 'c' needs to find all the other members of its family, as they seem to have got lost in letterland! Ask her to be a 'detective' and find the other members, or you may prefer to be more straightforward about your search! The only way to find the family is to feel all the other letters until you find one that makes the shape 'c' as you begin to feel it.

Feel the letter 'c' then choose another letter 'a' (pre-arranged in your pile). This begins in the same way as 'c'. Have your child feel the letter and discover that in fact 'c' and 'a' are related. Put 'a' on the table where the family will go. Feel 'c' again and choose another letter. Gradually the table fills up with all those letters that belong to 'c' and your pile of rejects gets put to one side.

**Here are the families that you should be able to find**

The 'c' family

c a d g q o


The 'r' family

r n m h b p

The 'i' family

i t l u y j k

The 'v' group

v w x

Certain letters will not fit into any group and these can be called the 'odd' family. Some letters, depending on the way you have drawn them, could belong to one of several families – 'k' for example, may belong to the 'r' rather than the 'i' family if it has a curved top. If you are using the templates from Chapter 9 for your Sandpaper Letters, the odd letters will be 'e' 'z' 'f' 's'.

Be guided by your child's decisions about the odd letters. Some children are happy to put 's' into the 'c' group because of the rounded shape made at the beginning and some children are happy for 'z' to belong to the 'v'

group because it contains a diagonal. As soon as a group of letters has been identified, feel through them as often as possible. Play the game often enough for your child to be able to sort out 'her' groups of letters very easily.

## Making letter shapes in sand
Age: around 3 ½ – 4 ½
**You will need**
A small tray or something similar – the lid of a biscuit tin will do, but don't use anything that has high sides. A small amount of fine sand, just enough to cover the base of the tray. If you don't have sand, and if you can stand the mess, you could try flour – your child will love it! Salt may be a better alternative but make sure she doesn't put her fingers in her mouth! A few Sandpaper Letters.

**Purpose**
This game will help your child to practise writing the shapes of letters, using her hand directly, before she begins to use a pencil to do so. Gradually her hand, using the model of the Sandpaper Letters, becomes more and more able to make a good attempt at writing the shape of letters.

**How to play**
Let your child choose a Sandpaper Letter that she can feel well. (You may want to limit the choice to those you know she can manage.) Take the letter of her choice to the table and put it beside the tray with the sand. Use the checklist opposite to make sure that her posture is good. Feel the Sandpaper Letter then show her how to make the same shape in the sand tray using your two 'writing fingers' (your first and middle ones), saying the sound out loud either as you trace it or immediately after-

RIGHT **Drawing Sandpaper Letters in sand is effortless and makes learning letters more interesting. Make sure your child follows the 'correct' movement when tracing the letters. (See the diagram on page 73.)**

## Checklist for writing

**Is her body relaxed and looking comfortable?**

Her feet should be on the floor, her back gently inclined and her body should not be twisted. If it is, check that the paper has not been overly slanted; slanting should really be left to the child to position the paper in a comfortable way.

**Is her hand able to travel easily across the paper?**

If more practice at using the hand lightly in other situations is required do more drawing and colouring, and more feeling of the Sandpaper Letters emphasizing 'lightness of touch'.

**Is her hand able to draw the pen/pencil across the paper?**

Is the paper in the right position? Does she have the right kind of pen or pencil? Is the size of her chair and table appropriate?

**Is the pencil/penhold comfortable and effective?**

Be flexible and observe what works for your child. Remember that her hands are a lot smaller than yours and unique in their own way. Try the alternative hold mentioned in this chapter and see if you find it comfortable too!

**Is the paper the right size?**

It shouldn't be too large to begin with, so that she can reach the top easily.

**Can she see what she is writing?**

Check the height of her chair, the light source and the size of her paper.

Lastly, make sure that any difficulties that are apparent are not caused by tension on the part of your child to succeed. Asking for perfect letter shapes before she is ready to form them will result in stress and tension, so only start 'writing' formally when she is ready – when she wants to write, rather than when you want her to. As a rule of thumb, she will be ready when she has sufficient pre-writing experience to be in control of her hands, when she is able to use tools such as paintbrushes, clay modelling tools, knives and forks properly and can dress herself. She must also be able to feel the Sandpaper Letters well, starting at the correct entry points and following the way in which the letter is written without any difficulty.

wards. Admire the result then gently shake the tray to make the letter disappear. Do the same thing over again a few times then ask her if she would like a turn.

Encourage her to repeat the 'drawing' of the letter as many times as possible before you go on to another letter. Always give your full attention to the start of the letter and encourage her to continue the movement of the letter appropriately. Try to leave her alone to explore the letter in sand. Make sure she always feels the letter first before she traces the shape in the sand. You may like to tell her that she can teach herself to write by feeling the letter. In this way she will experience a great sense of achievement.

### Feeling and writing the Sandpaper Letters

Once your child's hand can make a reasonably good attempt at tracing a shape in sand there are many other steps you can take to help her to develop good handwriting. It will be necessary to practice writing in conjunction with the Sandpaper Letters until her hand no longer needs to learn the correct way of making the shape; once this has happened the Sandpaper Letters are no longer useful.

I would recommend that you progress through the following games as appropriate to your child's developing skills. They will help her to master the following:

◆ Handling a writing implement.

◆ Controlling a writing implement on paper.

◆ Moving the writing implement in a particular direction and forming a particular shape.

◆ Producing letters that are uniform in size.

### Feeling and writing the sandpaper letters on a blackboard

Age: around 4 on

**You will need**

A set of Sandpaper Letters.

Chalk – different colours, but preferably not long, thin pieces as they break easily. Try to find chalk that is short and stubby. You may want to investigate dust-free chalk. Most good art shops will have these as will most good suppliers of children's toys.

A really good blackboard. You could use those that are often found on the other side of painting easels if you happen to have one at home, although there are some drawbacks to this. The movements that your child's arm, wrist and fingers make when writing on a surface, such as a table, is very different to the movements made when standing up at an easel. Standing up to practise writing isn't the best solution but may be the only one that you have to begin with. Ideally, you will buy or make a blackboard that is about A4 size. It should rest firmly on the table and should be heavy enough not to slip and slide about. The surface must not be shiny. Don't buy one from a shop until you have tried it out – amazingly shops do sell boards that are sometimes almost impossible to write on!

If all else fails you should go to your local ironmonger or DIY centre, or to your nearest educational supplier, and buy some blackboard paint. Any hard surface can be painted. A friend of mine painted the side of her washing machine. Her children had a wonderful blackboard to draw on and she felt that her ugly washing machine had been put to good use.

You will also need a really good blackboard rubber or a damp sponge.

**How to play**

Ask your child to choose a Sandpaper Letter that she likes and can feel easily. If she needs help, give her a choice of some letters in her name or any others that may have particular relevance for her. Place the letter slightly to one side of the board, making sure it will not twist her body into an awkward position when she feels it. Now you feel the letter, pick up the chalk and draw the letter on the board. Do it again several times; fill the board with as many attempts as you like, trying each time to form a beautiful shape. Now ask your child if she would like to do the same. Rub out your letters and let her start. In the beginning it doesn't matter where the letter is written on the board but encourage her to fill the board. The size of the letter doesn't matter either. After some time she will start to write the letters at a size that she feels comfortable with. When she has filled the board ask her to look at all the letters she has written and choose the ones she likes best!

Children have a clear idea of how they expect their letters to look and the blackboard provides a helpful start because any letter that your child is dissatisfied with can be rubbed out immediately if she doesn't like it. It's much better for her to practise on a blackboard before she moves on to paper.

### Writing letters on paper

Age: around 4 – 4½ on, when your child is confident about letters on a blackboard

When she starts to practice writing letters on paper she should be relatively happy with what she writes. Do not encourage the use of a pencil eraser.

**You will need**

A set of Sandpaper Letters.

You could offer a choice of colourful wax

crayons, similar in size to the chalk, or a limited choice of pencils and felt-tip pens. Don't have too many to choose from.

Plain (ie unlined) paper – this should be about A5 size and you could offer a range of colours. Make sure, however, that all the coloured crayons will stand out on the coloured paper.

### How to play

First make sure you have run through the checklist on page 92 regarding posture and the position of the paper. Then you could do any of the following:

◆ Encourage your child to feel and write the Sandpaper Letters as you did with the blackboard.

◆ Create a border around the edge of the paper and, when the middle has been filled in with beautiful letters, suggest to her that she decorate the border. You will have made a

ABOVE **Writing on lines using the Sandpaper Letters.**

BELOW **Drawing a border round her work and then decorating it will help your child feel proud of her work and will also help give her the idea of margins. And the middle can be used for a poem, a thank-you letter or a message.**

4th March

Dear Scilla,

Thank you for my lovely present.

Love Tom

modern day sampler!

◆ Choose one of the letter families (see Sorting into Families earlier in this chapter) and write all the letters from it on one sheet of paper. Repeat for the other families, each family occupying a separate piece of paper. Now encourage your child to write the families too.

◆ Observe her writing to see what size of letter she generally produces. Use this as a guide. Fold the paper over as if you were creating a concertina or fan – the width of the first fold to be determined by the size of her letters; the first fold should be about twice the size. If your child's letters are much too big to allow you to do this easily then she is not yet ready for this activity. A good indicator of size is often to look at the size that she writes her own name. Ask her to write her letters in a line, using the space between the folds. This activity should encourage her to start her letters on the left-hand side of the page and will help her to regularize their size. Please note that you are not asking her to write on the line, rather you are encouraging her to get letters moving in a line.

◆ If she finds it difficult to remember where to start, and this may be particularly difficult for a left-handed child, she could decorate the margin down the left-hand side of the page – you could make a simple bookmark and decorate it to fit on to the left-hand side of the page. You can do this easily by using a strip of card and cutting out a deep 'v' at the top – the 'v' can fit over the top of the page and remain relatively stable while she is writing). If your child is not interested in doing this, she might like to draw a coloured line down the side of the page to remind herself instead.

## Writing in the air

Have your child sit on your lap. Hold the hand that she writes with and draw a letter in the air, using her hand as the pencil. See if she can guess which letter you have written. Be sure you write in one smooth movement, starting the letter in the correct place. This is a great way of making sure that your child really 'feels' the way the letters are written.

## Finger painting the letters

If you were brave enough to organize finger painting to encourage pattern making in Chapter 3, it will be a natural step for your child to draw the shapes of the letters in the paint with her fingers, and to make a print of these on paper. Those she isn't satisfied with can be wiped away easily. Don't let her use the Sandpaper Letters as a guide for this activity – they're almost certain to get spattered! She will probably start to paint the the letters without any prompting from you but if she doesn't, only suggest it when you are fairly sure she can make a reasonable attempt at forming the shape without using the guide of the letter.

ABOVE **Your child will enjoy practising writing her letters if you can provide unusual and fun ways to help her do it.**

## Painting the letters

If your child enjoys painting you might like to provide her with smaller pieces of paper and a finer brush. She can sit at a table and paint letters on to paper. Once again, you would not really be wise to use the Sandpaper Letters as a guide as they will probably get painted inadvertantly! The main purpose of this should be to ensure that her hand is able to control the brush following the correct letter movement. The letters do not have to be perfect.

## Crayon and paint

Use really waxy crayons. Encourage her to write the letters on paper, then cover the paper with a light wash of paint and watch together as the letters appear through the paint.

## Gluing letters

### You will need

Water soluble glue. Either buy some or use wallpaper paste, which is cheap and easy to make. Use a paintbrush rather than a glue brush, which has a blunt edge. If you can find them, there are commercially available glue pens that work well with this activity.

You will also need glitter, sequins or sand and good-quality coloured paper. You may find it helpful to do this over a tray since it can be quite messy.

### How to play

Encourage your child to write letters in glue over the paper as quickly as she can. Now have her carefully sprinkle over the glitter, sequins or sand and shake. Watch as the glue letters appear.

## Drawing

As your child writes, carefully observe any difficulties she may have in forming the letters. Are some movements more difficult than others? Alongside her practice, encourage

more pattern making and still-life drawing as outlined in Chapter 3.

## Revisiting the sound and letter recognition games

If you look back at some of the games you played in Chapter 4, you will see that many can be adapted for your newly fledged author to write. For instance, she can label the pictures in the rhyming games you played; she can make her own alphabet book; she can start to use her own handwriting to send messages; and she can write lists and menus, and generally incorporate writing into her play.

## Worksheets and workbooks

You will have noticed, I hope, that I have avoided suggesting you provide dotted lines for children to trace over or use the many commercially available 'workbooks' on the market.

Schools often send children home with photocopied sheets on which to practise writing their letters (not good Montessori schools I hasten to add!). Many schools, because they have to teach large numbers of children to write at any one time, often are unable to give the kind of individual attention you can give to your child. Repetition does, of course, help children, but repetition that is boring will not help anyone. Sadly the problem with 'tracing' letters is that very often children do not trace them correctly in the first place. They take their hands off the letter at the wrong moment, have to conform to the size of letter on the sheets and the space provided for writing, and frequently these sheets are produced with print letters.

Your child's handwriting is unique and she should feel as proud to produce a beautiful letter as she does a beautiful drawing or painting. There should be no sense of duty attached to drawing letters. You can make practising her letters stimulating and fun by providing many different ways of doing it.

## Helping your child to control a pencil on paper

Age: around 4

You have encouraged your child to draw and colour-in pictures and you have also been helping her to explore patterns and shapes on paper. There is now one additional activity that you could introduce just as she is getting ready to do more controlled writing on paper. In a Montessori class it is called Metal Insets, although the children often call them mental insets or metal insects! It is possible to buy them, but you can just as easily make use of things around the house to achieve much the same effect.

### You will need

Some good-quality coloured pencils. Some good-quality plain (unlined) paper in lots of colours. An object, such as a small saucer or lid to draw around, or use insets from puzzles your child had when she was smaller. (These would be ideal if they were puzzles with knobs because the knobs would steady her hand.)

### Purpose

This activity will increase your child's control of the pencil on paper while practising techniques that will be required for writing.

### How to play

Have your child draw around the outside of the chosen shape as carefully as possible. This is quite difficult as her hand will tend to shoot off in different directions at the beginning. Then show her how to colour in the outline, moving the hand from left to right and flowing over the outline in an up and down movement that imitates the flow of the writing hand as it travels across paper. From quite long lines at the beginning you can start to colour in bands, then gradually introduce the idea of shading the outlines.

ABOVE **You can use any object, like this box, to draw a shape to help your child control a pencil on paper. After she has drawn the shape, encourage her to colour it in, using up and down strokes and travelling from left to right.**

Before you move on to help your child to write on lines, it may be useful to summarize the range of activities she is already engaged on:

◆ Writing creatively with the Moveable Alphabet – lists, stories, poems and messages.
◆ Practising writing letters using the Sandpaper Letters, through a number of different activities.
◆ Drawing and painting, and continuing to refine her hand control.
◆ Starting to use her own handwriting (as opposed to her earlier mark making) on her drawings, and she may use her own handwriting to send messages and write lists, menus etc. Many of the games you played earlier for sound and letter recognition can be played again at this point (see Chapter 3) and she will now be able to write her own letters.
◆ Continuing to be read to.
◆ Starting to read for herself.

## Helping your child to write on lines

Giving your child lines to help her to write and space well can be very useful, as long as you are prepared to adapt the size of the lines to the size of her writing. You will be able to judge what size the lines need to be if you check her writing on plain paper – a very good indicator is to look at the size she writes her own name.

There are various types of lined paper you can create to help her practise on, each with a slightly different purpose (see Chapter 9 for templates you can use). Choose which type you'd like your child to try but be prepared to change it if what you've chosen doesn't work. You will also need to change the size of the lines as her writing develops, until a single line is sufficient. Use A5 paper to start off with. Don't encourage her to use lines for all her writing, however; there will still be some things that are best written on plain paper.

The lined paper templates in Chapter 9 are each geared to provide a slightly different activity.

### Squared Paper

This provides a general guide for your child and will not limit the size of her letters.

### Shaded Line

This gives a guide for the main part of the letter and leaves the height of the ascenders and descenders to the child.

### Double line with darker base line

This focuses attention on the base line and gives guidance for the height of the main part of the letter.

### Four lines: colour coded

This gives guidance for ascenders and descenders as well as the main part of the letter.

## Placing letters on a line

Age: around 4 ½ – 5 on

Before you start the following activities your child should be able to make the correct movement of the letters by herself without needing to refer to the Sandpaper Letters unless there are still one or two that cause difficulty. She should also be keen and eager to write, and you must strike a balance between providing the necessary practice and making sure that the writing has some purpose. She should now be writing easily with the Moveable Alphabet.

### You will need

One of each of the letters of the alphabet – you can remove them from your Moveable Alphabet. If these are too large to fit on to your paper, reduce them on a photocopier. The letters will only be used for a short space of time in this activity so they don't need to be on card – paper should do.

Decide which type of lined paper you are going to try first; any of the templates – with the exception of the squared paper – will work. Take a large sheet of paper (A3 size would be about right), and draw the lines design you've chosen on to the paper, using the size of the letters you have made as your guide.

If you're using a two-line design the middle two lines should fit the 'c' size; if you're using a four-line design the top line should be at the height of the ascender in 'h' and the bottom line the depth of the descender in 'y'.

### How to play

*Sorting for size*

Explain to your child that she has been writing in lines and now you are going to show her where letters go when they are written on lines. Ask her to sort through all the letters and leave all the letters that fit between the 'shaded' or 'blue' lines on the paper. Those that do not fit should be put aside.

ABOVE **Discovering where to place letters on a line will prove valuable when your child comes to write on paper. This little boy has discovered letters that sit on the line and those that descend below it, and he will discover those that ascend above it.**

a  c  e  i  m  n  o  r  s  u  v  w  x  z

Clear these away after sufficient time has been spent looking at them.

Now ask her to sort out all the letters that have ascenders that go above the shaded area'or 'reach the top line.

b  d  h  k  l

Clear these away after sufficient time has been spent looking at them.

Sort out all the letters that have descenders that go below the shaded area or reach the bottom line.

g  j  p  q

You will be left with two odd letters – 't' which never quite catches up with the ascenders, and 'f' which may go above and below the main lines.

Now ask your child to mix up all the letters and see if she can sort them out according to size, placing them on the line as she goes.

Ask her to place all the letters on the lines at random and see if she can remember the placement of each letter.

*Sorting for families*

Ask her to sort the letters out on to the line but in their 'movement' families (see the Sorting into Families game, page 89). The letters that begin 'c', those that begin 'i', and those that begin 'r', then the odd ones.

*Writing on the lined paper*

Take some lined paper (A5 size) and ask your child to sort out the Moveable Alphabet letters in any of the ways outlined above. Using the sorted letters as a guide, she can write down the letters on the lined paper.

You must now find a variety of ways to help her practise writing using lines. Try to avoid asking her to repeat rows of a particular letter since this becomes very boring. You could choose groups of letters according to the way that they are written or 'move'. For instance, from the 'i' family movement group 'i' and 'l' could be practised together and 'u' and 'y' could be practised together. Explore the possibilities together, taking one family group at a time then look for similarities whether by 'movement' or by shape. The combinations are endless and all the time that you are studying the letters together her knowledge and awareness of the way letters are formed and written will be changing.

As she increases in confidence and speed she will want to write on the lines more often, and you will need to be sensitive to her needs and change the paper to suit her growing capabilities. Within a relatively short period of time she may be able to write all her letters on one line.

To assist this process, keep all kinds of paper available on a shelf so that she may choose the kind that suits her best, as different tasks will require different paper. She will want to begin to write down longer messages and stories, and gradually the attraction of the Moveable Alphabet dwindles as she finds she is able to write just as quickly by hand. Over the period of time between beginning to write with the Moveable Alphabet and being able to write well using her own handwriting, the erratic, purely sound-based spelling that she began with will gradually have changed, influenced by a number of different things. As she begins to read her awareness of the way words look when they are written down begins to change. She meets words that are not easy to sound out, and she meets words that she can recognize by looking at them as a whole. She will meet words that require some special knowledge to help her to crack the code, such as those ending in 'tion' or those that have a silent letter such as 'k' – knee, knot etc. You will see from the next two chapters that, as she has progressed in reading, you have encouraged her to become more careful about which letters make up particular words. At no time, however, during her work with the Alphabet have you emphasized correct spelling over self expression. Nevertheless, there will have been a subtle change in how she spells those words.

Once she is writing well on lines you can expect her spelling to be quite good. Watch out for very common words that are repeatedly mis-spelled, however, and show her how to write them. When she writes certain words by hand the form the words take can become a habit, and while not correcting all the spellings, you need to watch out for anything that might become a habit. The activities suggested in Chapters 6, 7 and 8 will all have an impact on spelling.

When your child first starts writing on lines it can be very helpful to provide her with some written models to follow, in addition to her own messages.

## Writing models

Age: around 4½ – 5½

### What you will need

Provide the paper your child seems most comfortable with – see the samples in Chapter 9. Write a variety of words, sentences, poems, jokes, messages that you think would appeal to her. These first examples will be relatively short but should increase in length and move on to different paper as her interests and needs develop. You will also be ready to 'scribe' anything that she may want to write with the 'proper' spelling. In this way, some of the examples will remain for a period of time while some will just be required once.

### How to play

You may like to begin with your child's name, which is always very special, or anything else you think she will feel like seeing written on the line, but do not begin with something that lasts longer than a line. Equally, don't reduce this to another 'drill', where words are simply copied without purpose or meaning. She has obviously been writing her name for some time but now you have an opportunity to show her what it looks like on a line.

Cut a strip from the writing paper and write her name, making sure that you are writing the letters with good movement.

Place your strip of paper directly above her own lines and ask her to copy it. Move the strip down as each line is completed. Once you have examples that are more than one line long you can either put them above her page or beside it. (To the left of a right-hander and the right of a left-hander so that they can see and write at the same time.)

Leave some paper strips with messages or names on an accessible shelf so that if she feels like writing and wants a ready prepared model to follow rather than her own thoughts, she has access to it at any time.

Some possible ideas for examples could be:

◆ Simple rhymes and poems that grow in length.
◆ The days of the week, months of the year.
◆ The families of letters.
◆ Letters grouped according to their size.
◆ The names of all the members of your family.
◆ Capital letters and lower-case letters side by side.

If your child is left-handed, you should attempt to write with your left hand too. And don't worry if it doesn't look all that good – it isn't the perfect shape of the letter that matters but the movement of the hand across the paper and the way the letters are formed that counts! If yours doesn't look all that wonderful encourage her to make a better job of it than you did. You can explain, if you need to, that you feel more comfortable writing with your right hand. If you are left-handed then you will have the opposite problem if your child is right-handed.

## Spacing

When helping your child to space her words it can be helpful, if she seems to need guidance, to suggest leaving a space between the words that is equivalent to one letter of the writing that she is doing normally. Do not suggest a finger space as this will cause small writing to be unnecessarily spaced out and large writing to be too close together.

## Capital letters

A simple explanation for a capital letter is that we use it when we wish to draw attention to something important, i.e. a name or the beginning of a new sentence.

Capital letters very rarely need to be taught – most children will pick up many of them from their everyday exposure to them: the M for McDonalds is just one example. Many capital letters are also very similar to their lower-case relatives. You may need to teach a few capital letters but your child will know the majority of them. Helping her to write them is also a much simpler task than helping her to learn to write lower-case letters as they are mostly, bar one or two styles, written using predominantly straight lines which can be written in a variety of ways.

What you may need to do is to teach the names of the letters to your child. Up until now, you will have mostly concentrated on the sounds, but once these are secure you can explain to her that the letters have a name as well as a sound.

Use any alphabet songs you know to link the names with the shapes of the letters. Invite your child to write the capital and lower-case letters belonging to, for example, 'D', giving the name and not the sound.

## Matching lowercase and capital letters
Age: around 5

BELOW **Make recognizing the differences between capital letters and lowercase ones into a game. When your child feels comfortable matching them, take away the control cards and ask him to do it from memory.**

Two sets of 26 alphabet cards, each of which has a capital letter followed by a lowercase letter. Take one set and cut it down the middle to separate the capital letter from the lower-case letter. You now have three sets of cards.

### How to play

Lay out the large cards, then take the capital letters and match them underneath the large cards. As they are laid down name the letter. Do the same for the lower-case letters. When this has been accomplished, play the game again, only this time lay out the capital letters first and match the lower-case letters to them without the guide. Use the large cards to check at the end to see if they are all matched up. If your child knows the order of the alphabet then she can sort them into the correct order.

Encourage her to practise writing capital and lower-case letters together, then watch as they gradually become used naturally in her writing. Be sure not to introduce capital letters until she has no difficulty writing the lower-case letters, however. In all the writing you have done in front of her you have used capital letters if they were appropriate, and through her reading and your example she will soon understand how to use them.

## More games to encourage writing
### Notice board

Put up a notice board at your child's height and leave her messages to read. Encourage her to write her own messages or answers to your messages on the board.

### Letters

Children love opening envelopes. Write her little messages and put them into an envelope with her name on. Make sure you also provide some envelopes on her writing shelf so that she can write letters to you.

## Books

You can now begin to write real books together. Look at a real book and discover what you will need to do. Where does the title appear? What is on the inside cover? Will you need pictures? What will the story be about? Don't be too ambitious in the beginning – some very good stories can be written with very few words. Perhaps your child would like to make a little diary for herself, recording one particular event that she remembers a day? Encourage her to make cards to send to friends and family.

ABOVE **Helping your child to put pictures into sequences can be an early start to writing stories. Once you've assembled the pictures in the right order you can make up a story to go with them – and even make it into a book!**

# CHAPTER SIX

# Starting to read

Arriving at the moment when your child is ready to read is very exciting for all concerned. By now you will have made sure that she has had many different experiences with words which, together, have created in her a readiness to read.

◆ *You have given her knowledge of the world.* Through taking her out and about and engaging her in lots of conversation you have given her experience of the world. You have used language richly and well, and attached it to real life and real life experiences so that when she reads words, situations and predicaments will have some resonance.

◆ *You have given her a knowledge of books.* She understands the importance of print to convey stories and the rhythms and forms that stories take. She knows how to handle books. She feels a sense of ownership of some of her precious books and will choose to look at them even when there is no prospect of someone reading to her. She has experienced the pleasure that can be had from reading or being read to. By sharing books with you she has learned to recognize some words already without any effort.

◆ *She has a good knowledge of sounds, rhymes and sound clusters.* She has learned these through the many songs, poems and nursery rhymes you have recited together, through the various sound games you have played with her and through learning symbols that are attached to these sounds.

◆ *She has become an author herself.* Through writing down messages and stories with the Moveable Alphabet, she understands that print conveys her thoughts, that words are sound units that can be strung together into meaningful units, and that she is able to read what she herself has written.

◆ *She feels like a reader.* Having written her own messages and read them, having 'read' many stories and having a family where books are valued, your child will feel that she is a reader and will be eager and ready to have a go at reading more and more.

How can you help to get her started? The ability to read will depend on her being able to do a number of different things at once. Perhaps the first question you must ask yourself is this. 'Why should she choose to read'?

Reading should be an enjoyable experience because what she reads interests her and gives her a sense of accomplishment. It gives her more autonomy in what she can find out for herself and a greater sense of independence. She will be able to discover things for herself and she will be able to take herself off into 'other worlds', in which what she reads has only her own imagination as its limit. She wants to read because reading has a purpose for her. The reading that you do with her must then be of interest to her. It cannot simply be reading for reading's sake.

Don't be tempted to buy a set of 'basal readers' or 'primers' to help you through this stage. The value of these books is usually only to help a teacher know what level of reading a child can do. All too often they rely on very limited language, which is often far removed from either real language or real book language, with stilted rhythms and awkward word sequences. The limited nature of the vocabulary can often make the flow of the words boring. It is also rare to find content that actually interests children of this age in these books. Although there are some that are above average, having to read through 25 books all about the same family can be extremely boring after a while!

Children rarely return again and again to these books and they hold no real pleasure for them other than to encourage a competitive element to reading. Rather than discussing the content of these books with each other, children tend to discuss what number or colour level they have reached. Recent research has revealed that although these books try to focus on a limited vocabulary, ordinary story books in fact give a child far more practice at the most commonly used words.

When children read they will use a variety of strategies to help them understand what they are seeing. They will, for example, rely quite heavily on any clues they can pick up from the surrounding words, pictures or situation: we call this the context. A child coming across the word 'kangaroo' may look at the picture for help; if she doesn't find it much help she may use her knowledge of the situation and her ability to predict what may follow on from it as a natural consequence.

She will also rely on her knowledge of the world to help her to predict what a word is likely to mean. We know when we come across a word that could have a variety of meanings such as 'bear' the mind presents itself with a choice of all possible meanings known to the reader. In a split second, before you are even aware of it, the mind is able to choose what it believes is the most suitable meaning for the context. The wider your child's experiences and vocabulary, the more options will pop into her mind and the more likely she is to find the meaning that fits the sentence.

She will also use her own natural understanding of language to help her guess what might be coming next, what would make sense and what any given word might be. As she reads, she uses her intrinsic knowledge of grammar to help her to get to the meaning of the words that she is reading. A very good example of how we use our knowledge of language to help us to crack the meaning of a sentence can be found in the wonderful nonsense rhyme by Edward Lear 'The Jabberwocky'. The first lines read like this:

*'Twas brillig, and the slithy toves*

*Did gyre and gimble in the wabe,*

Many of these words are not used in the English language. But can you pick out the words that describe the action? Can you discover the subject of the sentence? We may not recognize the words but our understanding of our language can help us to go some way towards unravelling the meaning of the sentence. When we search for meaning in these lines we try to imagine what 'slithy toves' would look like and then what actions best fit 'gyre and gimble'. I use this poem simply as an illustration and not because I think you should use it for your children to read at this stage!

Play the following games to launch your child easily and relatively effortlessly into reading. You can play them at the same time as you begin to share the reading of books together. They are designed to help her practise putting sounds together to make up words, which will enable her to read more fluently.

## Reading using objects

Age: from around 4 ½ on – you will begin to play this game when your child first starts reading words that she has written on her own with the Moveable Alphabet.

This game relies on your child having enjoyed the Sound Game, the Sandpaper Letters and the Moveable Alphabet. You aren't going to teach her anything new playing it; you will simply build on her past experiences and knowledge gained from these three games.

Your child already knows that sounds can

**Writing down the names of favourite toys or other objects in front of your child will help her make the connection between objects and sounds, and writing and reading.**

be represented by written symbols and that by placing these down in a particular order words are made. She has also begun to blend these sounds together for herself and read her own writing.

### What you will need

Two different sets of small objects (have at least eight things); they could be gathered from around the house or you could visit a toyshop or a shop that sells miniatures, if you really want to push the boat out! The objects that you collect should all be objects of desire and they do not need to relate to one another.

The first set should be objects that are phonetically spelt, that is, where each sound in the word is represented by one letter only so that as it is sounded out, it can be blended together to create the name of the object without any distortion or change to the sounds.

Assuming you did a quick round of the kitchen and your child's bedroom you could end up with the following objects:

| | | | | |
|---|---|---|---|---|
| cup | lid | lamp | pot | nut |
| pen | lemon | van | jug | drum |
| milk | pasta | banana | panda | dog |
| comic | nutmeg | melon | tin | mug |
| cap | hat | bag | clip | vitamins |

As you can see, you don't have to stick to three-letter words; a few would be helpful but don't try to use this game to move from three-letter words to four-letter words and so on.

You could also introduce words that have double letters in them after a short while, such as carrot, doll, bell, clock, egg, brick (although the 'c' and 'k' look different, the sound that they make is the same).

The second set of objects should be objects that contain a digraph in them (those that your child already knows from the Sandpaper Letters). In every other respect the words can be sounded out like the objects in the first set.

Examples could be:

| | | | | |
|---|---|---|---|---|
| train | cloth | brush | ketchup | toy |
| star | book | letter | fork | coffee |
| pie | coat | blue | quilt | trout |

As soon as your child has read these a few times, you could introduce words which have more than one digraph such as sweetcorn, squash or cheese (the silent 'e' doesn't present a difficulty as it doesn't alter the way any of the other letters sound).

If you want to make a game that she can go back to, you may want to shop around for little objects to supplement what you have at home. Montessori schools have little boxes for this game with all sorts of delightful objects in them, which enables them to change the objects around so that the children are always interested to read what is in them.

If you were really stuck, you could always just collect pictures of objects, but the objects themselves are much more fun.

You will also need some paper strips and a pencil so that you can write the names of the objects down.

### Purpose

The purpose of playing this game is to help your child realize how easily she can put together the sounds that she already knows and read them – the objects are used to create a 'context' for her. She will know that the word has to be from the group of objects in front of her and this should help her to read the labels you will give her.

### How to play

One of the most important elements of this game is that you are going to write down the names of the objects in front of your child so that she sees your thought literally translated on to paper in front of her eyes. The underlying message you are conveying is that when we read we are reading the thoughts of someone else. The fact that written words are always the product of someone's thought is important; it gives value to the written word and links together the writing and reading processes. Your child will value the little labels you write for her to read far more than she does ready-prepared labels.

Collect the first phonetic set of objects together, either on the floor or on a table. (A table would be preferable because you are going to write.)

**Vocabulary check**

Make sure your child knows the names of all the objects you are using. If you have chosen a toy cat and she uses the word 'kitty' to describe it you will need to give her the name you will use for the game.

'Well, that is your "kitty" but for this game we need to call it "cat".' You couldn't use the word kitty because it is not phonetic.

Write your thoughts down for your child to read

Tell your child you are thinking of one of the objects on the table. Ask her if she knows which one it is. Some children will pick up an object straightaway and if she does, do not accept it as the object you were thinking of.

'Well, that is not the one that I was thinking of. Let me give you a clue'.

Some will ask for a clue from the outset. Write, in handwriting that is beautiful and matches the style that you have chosen to teach your child, the name of the object you wanted.

'This is what I wanted'.

Let your child see you write down the letters on a strip of paper. In this way she will see the connection between what you are thinking and what she will be reading.

## Sounding out

Give your child the strip of paper and ask her to sound out what she sees on it. She will begin to make the sounds and you should encourage her to run them together faster and faster until, with a combination of blending sounds and looking to see which of the objects it may relate to, she will identify the object. Be absolutely delighted and exclaim that she knows what you are thinking of because she

was able to read your message. Put the object and the label together and continue until all the objects have been labelled.

You will observe that she will partly be 'reading' the words and partly using the objects as 'context'. She knows that what is written relates to the choice of objects placed in front of her. She will combine a variety of strategies to read the word in front of her – sometimes she will use an educated guess (what object is left that begins with 'p', for example), sometimes she will sound it out completely.

## Repetition and confirmation

Ask your child to read over all the objects and their labels. This will help her to focus on the word as a whole. She will, of course, know the object and will then 'read' the word easily. It helps if she can point to each label as she says it, bringing her eye to a view of the whole word.

You will tire of this game long before she does. If you want to see if she can do the activity by herself you could prepare some labels for her to use. If she is writing she could write her own labels for the objects. Don't expect her to read the labels without any contextual clues. She may be able to do so but you should not suggest it.

## Reading the digraphs

You can introduce the second set of objects containing the digraphs as soon as your child finds it easy to read the first set: this could be the next day or the day after for some children. You must remember that she doesn't have to learn anything new to do these games. She only has to apply the knowledge she has already gained from the Sound Game and the Sandpaper Letters, and use her experiences with the Moveable Alphabet and the reading that you have been doing with her.

Do exactly the same with the second set of objects as you did with the first. However, when writing your message underline the two letters that between them make a single sound – for example, book.

Depending on your child, you might want her to identify the underlined sound before trying to sound out the letter. As you continue to write the labels, according to your child's ability, stop underlining and have her identify the digraph on her own.

If you would like to make this activity more permanent you could collect little objects that you have found in shops or from among her toys and keep them in a box with the words that were originally written by you inside. Add different objects and their labels from time to time to keep her interested in looking inside.

## Reading without using objects

Many of the words that describe actions in English can be written using only Sandpaper Letters and digraphs. You can make up some very interesting words that your child will be able to read and act out very easily – she will love acting out the different words you have written and in doing so she will have to demonstrate that she has understood their meaning.

### What you will need

Write out on small cards as many different 'action' words as you can think of that can be read using only Sandpaper Letters and the digraphs. (You will be using the same knowledge your child employed to play the two previous reading games.) There should be only one action word per card. This time, however, there are no objects to provide a 'context': her experience and the fact that she will act out the words on the cards should help her test out her understanding of the meanings.

Here are a few suggestions to get you started. You will note that some are easy to read and to do and others require a little more interpretation. If she gets stuck with the interpretation of a card, you will also need to act it out! Don't simply read the cards; they have almost no value unless they are acted out.

Words that could be written on the cards include:

| | | | | | |
|---|---|---|---|---|---|
| jump | run | hop | skip | stand | wink |
| blink | think | drink | yawn | sit | spin |
| grunt | moan | drag | rip | tap | hug |
| sleep | grin | clap | sing | groan | tap |

### How to play

You can either write these down as you go along or have them ready prepared. As with all the other activities, it would be better if you wrote them down as you went along, then kept them in a box so that your child can return to them when she feels like it.

Explain to her that you are going to write down some words and the important thing about them is that she must do what they say. Write 'run'. Your child reads the word and you encourage her to do the action. When she returns, write another word. Continue until she has had enough. You will find that reading these words leads into all kinds of discussions. Be as dramatic as possible.

## Writing sentences to be interpreted

If you have a child who loves acting out you could extend this activity into one in which you write out different sentences for her to read, interpret and do.

For instance:

Fetch your best doll/car/book

Find a green marble/red sock/blue cup

ABOVE **Play an 'action' game with your child to help him develop his reading skills.**

RIGHT **The better he can read, the more complicated (and fun) the messages can become!**

Tickle Dad/Mum/Gran/Grandpa

Pretend you are a doctor

Put your toys in the basket

Run your bath

Find three things for us to munch

Plant a seed

Fix your truck

Put on some music.

This game can go on all morning – perhaps even all day. The amount of enjoyment gained from reading these simple sentences is immense. Be prepared for the game to be reversed so that you are on the receiving end of messages from your child!

These activities should give your child lots of confidence when reading with you. There are some suggestions for the kind of books you might like to read with her in Chapter 9, although you should always remember that she will be most keen to read what she is interested in, even if this means that she will choose books that look too hard for her. If this is the case for your child, use some of the tips offered later in this chapter to help her accomplish it. I have watched children learn to read subject matter at levels of reading that were much harder than I would have chosen for them.

From this point onwards you will see that her ability to read will progress in leaps and bounds, followed by periods of calm. On your trips to the library, your librarian should be encouraged to offer books that reflect the level of reading and interest that your child has. Be wary of the librarian or bookshop assistant that points you in the direction of a particular reading scheme!

If your language is a phonetic one, you can jump forward to towards the end of this chapter, which deals with helping your child to read books. But if your first language is English, which is non-phonetic, you need to consider how you can help her to recognize quickly some of the words that cannot be sounded out, and you should therefore read on.

### Recognizing common words that cannot be sounded out (Puzzle Words 1)

Age: just after you have first introduced the reading boxes above and while your child is still enjoying doing them. This will be the first game you have played in a while that is going to offer something totally new to learn.

#### Purpose

As with every other activity in this book, the aim here is not to try to provide every difficult word that your child may come across in the course of her early attempts at reading. We will try to choose some common ones that it would be useful to know so that, once again, while she is reading she can recognize these words and extract the meaning of the sentences she reads more easily. To try to give too many would create more difficulties than it would solve.

Visualize your child as a hang-glider, not as a mountain climber. She is at this moment gliding through the air, making use of the different thermal currents, ascending effortlessly and discovering views and vistas that have until now been beyond her reach. She uses what she needs to extend and expand her horizons. There never was a mountain to climb. As she has progressed along the path to literacy, she has enjoyed each game for its own sake and not because it was another peak to climb, and she has arrived without ever knowing she set out. There have been no failures and no difficult goals, just an exploration of language in verbal and written form.

The words that cannot easily be sounded out we call puzzle words because they're such a puzzle!

### What you will need

You will need to discover which words are impossible to sound out yet appear most often in the books your child will be reading. Below I have given some ideas for you to draw on. Choose about ten or twelve at the most and make them up into individual cards.

| To | be | we | he | by | the | are |
| you | any | your | they | was | some | my |
| like | here | do |

### How to play

Choose about three of the words you wish to focus on; make sure that they are very different in the way they sound and look.

Tell your child that these words are quite puzzling because we cannot sound them out – try sounding out the word 'your' for example. Explain to her that she must simply be able to recognize these words when she sees them, and that it will really help her to read if she knows what they are.

You are once again going to follow the model of the three period lesson, first discussed in Chapter 2 (see page 37). This is how you could go about it. Before you start, you will need to make sure what the words mean and you can do this as follows:

◆ Today you can learn to recognize some words that are difficult to sound out. Here is one of them. (You write the word 'your', using the same style of script as the Sandpaper Letters, on a strip of paper.)

◆ This says 'your'; we can't sound it out very easily, shall we try? (You try, but it comes out as yu o u ru. This may amuse her! Now put the word 'your' into a sentence so that she hears it in context. 'Your dress is very pretty'. 'Your favourite colour is purple'. 'I like your cheeky grin',

◆ Put the word aside and repeat the same thing with the other two words, 'the' and 'like'.

*Stage 1*

Point to each of the words again and repeat the word clearly. Encourage your child to repeat it too –'your' 'the' 'like'

*Stage 2*

Ask questions:

Which word says 'your'?

Can you read 'like'– make sure she looks at the correct card.

Put the word 'the' over here – return it to the middle of the table.

Point to 'like'.

Continue with this stage until it seems easy for your child to read the words. Encourage her to repeat the words as often as possible after you have said them; you aren't asking her to remember them at this moment, simply to associate the names with the way they look on the paper.

*Stage 3*

You ask your child if she can read the words. At this stage you are careful not to say the word unless she gets stuck, in which case simply say it out loud and know that you will try again with this one on another day.

Can you read this? Do you know what this one says?

This lesson should take no longer than five minutes. Keep all the puzzle words that you make up in a little box as you will need them for the activities that follow.

### Reading sentences using the word that has just been learned

You should encourage your child to read the word in sentences. To begin with you could write some simple sentences with the words she has just learned.

> **Your** dress is red. Have **your** lunch. Find **your** doll.

> **The** kettle is hot. Find **the** marbles. Is your book on **the** table?

> Your rabbits **like** carrots. Mum and Dad **like** books.

You can fetch a book that you are reading together and start to find the new words that she can read.

## Writing sentences using the word that has just been learned

### Using the Moveable Alphabet and puzzle words

Encourage your child to put out the letters of the puzzle words with the Moveable Alphabet so that she focuses on each letter and its sequence in the word.

See if, after a while, she can read the word, turn the puzzle card face down and put out the Moveable Alphabet letters in sequence from memory. You could make this much harder by putting the puzzle word cards in another room to see if she can still remember how to put the Alphabet letters out when the lapse of time is greater between reading and writing them.

When she is writing spontaneously with the Moveable Alphabet you can encourage her to refer to the puzzle words if she forgets how they go. If they are spelled incorrectly you can gently remind her that she knows how to write the words, and either help her to sequence the letters correctly or suggest she

finds the puzzle word that you wrote. Slowly and gently the words that she is writing with the Alphabet will begin to become closer to the accepted conventional spelling of your language.

### Using paper

Her new-found knowledge should also have an effect on anything she is writing down using her own handwriting. You could suggest that she might like to copy the words on to some lined paper, if she is at the lined paper stage in writing. Beware, however, of creating a boring activity for her to do – always try to ensure that there is real purpose and meaning to each one; anything 'mindless' soon leads to the feeling that writing is a chore! You could include the words that she has learned in sentences that she dictates to you and which she can then copy.

## Treasure hunt

This is a simple variation on the adult game. Write simple clues to lead your child from one place to the next until she finds the 'treat' you

RIGHT **The so-called 'Puzzle Words' (see page 112) often create problems. One way to help your child to become more familiar with them is to create individual puzzle word cards and encourage her to use the Moveable Alphabet to 'match' them.**

have hidden. Clues such as 'Look in your boots', 'Go to the kitchen', 'Open the drawer' would all make use of the words she had come to recognize. And if you want further inspiration, follow the clues in the photograph!

## Reading together

You have been reading to your child every day since she was tiny, and you have watched her develop a love of books. You have watched her begin to recognize some words in the familiar and much loved books that you have shared. She now chooses books to read to herself and pores over the pages on her own. Her use of language has grown and she is now able not only to speak well, but also to write down her thoughts using the Moveable Alphabet and to some extent in her own handwriting, and has begun to read these too. She can read most phonetic words and those with digraphs, and is extending her knowledge of puzzle words. The reading that you do together now will gradually change in balance: her reading will increase as yours decreases with certain books. You will certainly not stop reading to her but you also need to find time for the two of you to read together, and you will now begin to choose books that you can read together. This will probably mean revisiting some of your old favourites and looking out for new books that will hold interest for her.

Here are some tips for getting started:

### Your attitude

◆ Reading should always be a pleasure, never a chore.

◆ Never force your child to read.

◆ Choose a time when she is not tired.

◆ Ask her to choose a book she would like to read, or offer her a choice of books and respect her choice.

◆ Encourage and praise whenever necessary; don't insist on perfection.

ABOVE **A treasure hunt can be educational as well as fun. Write out simple messages for your child and hide them around the room to find – and read. The final clue to this treasure is in the mug.**

RIGHT **The more you read, the more your child (or grandchild) will want to read.**

◆ Don't set any kind of timescale – 10 minutes of concentrated reading is better than half an hour of nagging.

### Choosing books

You will want to have the right kind of books available to get off to a good start and so, in addition to your old favourites, you may decide to go to the library and come back with a selection, or visit your local bookshop.

◆ Choose books that have a strong story line. Too much description in the beginning is not helpful.

◆ Choose old favourites or new books that you know your child will be interested in.

◆ Choose books where the illustrations clearly complement the text; this will help her obtain extra clues from the pictures.

◆ Choose books whose content falls within her experiences. She should understand what the book is about and be able to predict the likely events.

◆ Choose books that don't have too many

sentences to a page.

◆ Remember that children love humour.

◆ Books with large print are not necessarily easier to read; choose the book for the content and the pleasing layout of the text.

◆ Some books are written with text on two different levels, both belonging to the story. Very often the story text runs along the page and the pictures have simpler speech bubbles that relate to the text – this can be very successful when sharing a book.

◆ Don't exclude comics and books about facts – don't just read fiction.

◆ Rhyme and rhythm play an important part in helping children to predict what may come next.

### Giving the right help

◆ It's helpful to run your finger smoothly under the text as you read, and it may help your child to do the same. If she has difficulty in differentiating the lines then a strip of paper held under the line she is reading may help.

◆ Do nothing at all if your child mis-reads a word but gets the sense of the sentence right. She might substitute the word 'supper' for 'dinner'. This is fine; she is reading for meaning and the meaning of the sentence isn't altered.

◆ If she makes a mistake in the meaning, wait until she has finished the sentence and see if she corrects herself. If she doesn't, you could ask if the word she used sounded right. Return to the sense of the sentence and see if she can identify the word correctly.

### If she is stuck on a word

If she's stuck on a word try and judge which of the following would be the most helpful for her. The most important thing is to keep the flow of the story going and so you don't want to stop too often. If she is making so many mistakes that it affects the rhythm and pace of the story, you may wish to read with her to lessen any frustration she

may begin to experience.

◆ Supply the word so that the flow of the story continues and she isn't unduly worried about the odd word that she cannot read.

Perhaps she would benefit from your using one of the following clues to help her to read the word – you will be the best judge of which one might be most helpful. If the one you choose doesn't work simply tell her the word rather than continuing to dwell on what she doesn't seem to know.

◆ You could ask a question about what has gone before in the text.

◆ You could ask her to predict what she thinks it might be.

◆ You could help her to sound the word out; if it's a long one you may need to break it up into syllables.

◆ You could refer to the picture; if the word is actually in the picture you could simply point to it.

Remember that praise and encouragement go a long way to supporting your child when she is learning something new. Don't be tempted to criticize her reading or measure her against other siblings. It can be so easy to destroy the confidence that she needs if she is to become a successful reader.

## More games to play

There are lots of commercially available games that will build on the skills your child has acquired in this chapter – see Chapter 9 for a list of recommended ones.

## Book making

In almost every chapter of this book I have encouraged you to make books with your child and this one is no exception. By now she can be encouraged to write in her own words – and the more she does this the easier it will be for her to read 'her' book.

# CHAPTER SEVEN

# Reading for meaning

Your child is now reading and writing, and she is choosing books to read with you and spontaneously writing little stories and messages. You will see her pore over books by herself, watch as her lips move silently, working out words that she gets stuck with. She has a number of strategies that she can call upon as she reads, and when she gets into difficulty she knows that she can ask you to help if she really cannot understand a word she comes across. As she begins to read simple books on her own, you can sometimes discuss the story with her as a way of discovering how much she has managed to understand the story line.

You enjoy going to the library with her when you can, and time passes easily when you visit the bookshop.

You will not now have to worry about helping her to read or write, and can turn your attention to seeing if you can play some games with her that will make reading and writing even more enjoyable.

Words not only need to be read with the eyes they almost need to be tasted if we are really to enjoy using them. The activities that follow here will help your child get a lot more from the words themselves: they will focus both on improving fluency and helping her get a feel for what words do and how they do them. As a result these activities should raise her ability to interpret what she reads and help her to become more playful with words when she writes.

## Activities to help fluency and spelling

When reading English there are some helpful clues that we can offer as regards the many ways sounds can be written down.

If we think of the sound 'ai' for example, it can be written as in train, play, cake, vein. Having given your child a start by including the digraph 'ai' as a 'key sound', you could find a way of helping her to begin to read other forms of 'ai' quite quickly.

Look all the way through the Sandpaper Letters your child knows, remembering the sound they make, and choose those that are commonly spelled in more than one way. For instance, from the list below 'ai' can be spelled as in play (ay), cake (cake) and vein (ei).

### Key sound envelopes 1

Age: around 5

Some key sounds that can be spelt in different ways:

| | |
|---|---|
| ai | a-e, ay, ei |
| ee | ea, e-e, y, ie |
| ie | igh, i-e, y, |
| oa | ow, |
| ue | oo ew u-e |
| f | ph |

| | |
|---|---|
| e | ea |
| j | ge/gi dge |
| s | ci/ce |
| or | au, aw, |
| er | ir, ur |
| ou | ow |

You will need to make some cards or little paper strips for the alternative ways of spelling the key sounds. Write each sound on a card or strip and on the back put the key sound in small letters in another colour. Put each pack into a little envelope and mark the front of the envelope with the key sound.

Now put a little book of paper strips into the envelope. Each paper strip 'page' of the book should carry a small sentence containing a number of words with the sound in it.

For example in the 'ai' folder you might have:

As the **mail train** left the platform, it started to **rain**

Every **day** we **play** hide and seek and then run aw**ay**.

Let's bak**e** a cak**e** and then mak**e** some biscuits.

Finally, put little packs of words written with the alternative spellings into the envelope. For instance,

Train, rain, mail, tail

Make, bake, cake, crate

Vein, skein, freight

Play, stay, day, away

### How to play

Bring out an envelope and ask your child to recognize the key sound you have written on the outside.

Explain that all the cards inside the envelope are going to say the same sound. Look at the

ABOVE **Learning to recognize the different ways that a digraph like 'ai' could be spelled is fun in the Key Sound Envelopes game.**
RIGHT **Once you've learned to recognize the individual digraph words in the Key Sound Envelopes you can go on to read the sentences in the little booklets that were inside the envelopes.**

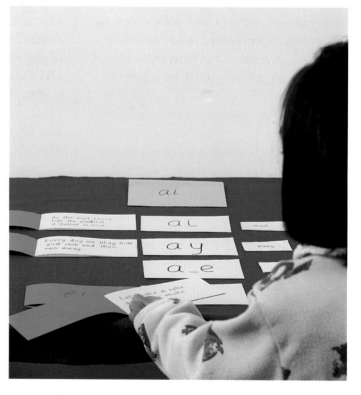

different ways that they are written.

Take out the pack of little words and read through the words, putting them next to the key sound.

Take out the little booklet and read through it.

She will find this activity relatively easy to do and you should compliment her on how well she is able to manage. You should also keep drawing attention to the different ways in which the sound can be spelled.

Do this for as many envelopes as your child would like. This activity can be spread over many days so there's no need to prepare all the packs at once, although it's nice to be able to offer her a choice of which key sound she would like to explore.

If you need to explain the 'a-e' card, make some additional cards that explain how it works: for instance cap becomes cape and tap becomes tape.

### Next step

Invite her to write out the words and the sentences if she wishes, either using her own handwriting or the Moveable Alphabet. If she likes she can use the envelope words as a memory guide. Mix the words up together and write some nonsense rhymes ensuring that the word is spelled using the correct 'ai' spelling.

You will notice that having become aware of the different ways in which this sound can be spelled when she is writing, she will begin to ask which 'ai' is it for play.

### To help her to remember

When she has read a number of the envelopes, take two or three together and take out the cards or strips. Mix them all up and see if she can sort them back underneath the envelope they belong to. She will be able to check herself by turning over all the cards to see the key sound written on the back.

This game is quite important to play, as she

will discover that the letter 'y' can say 'ie' and it can also say 'ee', e.g. 'sky' and 'party' and that the letters 'ea' can say 'ee' and also 'e', e.g. 'teach' and 'bread'. This is the reverse discovery to the one she made earlier: first she looked at sounds that were spelled differently, now she is discovering that some letters can have more than one sound too.

Once the cards can be sorted out, mix up the words from the different packs and encourage her to write some more sentences or stories using these words.

### Puzzle Words 2

Age: around 5

You may already have made a set of Puzzle Words in Chapter 6 (see page 111). This variation of the original game will build on your child's increasing interest in the way in which words are formed – the Key Sound Envelope game above will have helped stimulate this.

For this game you will need to make a second set of puzzle words which this time will focus on common patterns in words that, once learned, can be applied to a wide range of other words (see Chapter 9).

Choose some of the following to make into this second set:

could

through

all – call, fall, hall

air – fair, hair, chair

silent K – knee, knot, knit

silent B – lamb, thumb, comb

silent W – write, wrong, who

tion – station, nation

This set of puzzle words is to show small rules that may be useful for her to know. Begin by isolating the card that you want to be the archetype: e.g. 'all', 'air', 'tion'. Choose three at any one time and introduce them as you did the other puzzle words – first by putting them into context then by following the three period lesson. Make sure you examine the letters to see how they go together.

When your child is able to read these three archetypes, introduce others that are like it. For example 'Now that you can read "air" can you read "fair", "lair" "hair".' Either have already-prepared cards for these or simply write them down and see if your child can think of any. It will be easy for her to come up with rhymes but more difficult for her to understand which words have silent letters.

### Classified cards and labels

To help increase your child's fluency, it can be helpful to make use of the cards that you used originally for developing vocabulary. Write the name of the object on each card on the back

of it and make a label that is separate. Put out the cards and ask your child to read and match as many of the labels as she can to the cards. She can turn them over to check if she has read them correctly: if the words match she knows she's got it right.

### Naming the house

You could write all the names of the objects in different rooms of the house for her to read – using post-it notes for this is fun and very convenient. You write and she reads. After a while she will want to write too.

### Using books

Another way of extending this experience is to go back to the books that you used with her when she was around 18 months to two years old. Many of them were single pictures on a page with a word underneath. Cover over the words with post-it notes and write labels on more post-it notes. She can read and match the names. There are some wonderful books that you can buy that are designed for increasing vocabulary in particular subject areas – see the list in Chapter 9.

## Reading for meaning

Your child has an intrinsic knowledge of grammar and syntax and how words work together. It is amazing that formal grammar and syntax lessons can become so boring and obtuse that most of us believe that we cannot do it. Having an understanding of the

**LEFT Write words that identify furniture and objects around the room and ask your child to read them and stick them on to the items. Don't use strong stickers; they're sometimes difficult to remove afterwards! Post-its work well.**

way words work for us, and what they do, will help us get the 'taste' of what we read and will give us the opportunity to play with words.

You should have no intention of teaching grammar to your child. At this stage it is not only unnecessary but even undesirable. What we can do, however, is to give her a direct experience of what words can actually do, to explore how they work. The preparation you provide at this stage is simply to give experience on a level at which she can have fun. As you are aware, the way that her mind works means that these experiences are not lost and they will help to support and bolster the more formal ideas she will be presented with at a later date. The following activities are designed to give an extra experience to help her appreciate the way words can be made to work.

They are done based on her own previous experiences with language and involve manipulating objects or putting her into different situations, some with dramatic overlay.

## Using descriptive words

Age around 5 – 6

### What you will need

Use one of the following: a child's farm, dolls' house, garage collection, Playmobil people, Barbie doll or Action-man gear – in short anything that belongs together. Also make sure that there are several copies of some objects but that they look a little different – for instance, if you have a garage you will need some of the following: large van and a small one, a red van and any other colour of van, a heavy van and a dirty/clean van; a fast car, a racing car, a yellow car, any other colour car. You don't need several types of all the objects but there should be more groups of objects than single objects.

You will also need paper and scissors, and two pens or pencils, one an ordinary colour like blue or black (or lead), the other a bright colour not usually used for writing: red, orange, purple.

### How to play

Tell your child she is going to be able to find the very object you are thinking of without any difficulty. Think very hard and write down a message for her. This message says 'The van'.

Your child reads the message and collects a van from the garage. You agree that it is a van but not the one you were thinking of. Tell her that you will give her another clue. In a different colour pen write down the missing word that will identify the object. It could be 'red' or 'old' or 'broken', whichever identifies the van best. She will read the word. Chop the original label in half and put the new word into the middle of the phrase: you now have 'The old van'. Your child has no hesitation in choosing the appropriate object. Do this for several other objects. She will always ask you to put in the special word that helps her to find one object from many similar objects. You can continue writing down descriptions of all the objects for her to read; for example, if there is only one man you can now write 'The busy man' rather than just 'The man'. Try to use lots of different types of descriptions for the objects – it's very easy to stick with just colour and size so see if you can be a bit more imaginative than that. Use words such as grumpy, dilapidated, kind, gentle, angry, to really stretch her understanding of this type of word. You have the ideal opportunity to discuss them with her.

## Discovering how important word order is

This activity is hilarious for children to play. Adults don't always quite appreciate the humour that children find in nonsense! Take one of your strips of paper and mix up the word order. The old van becomes: old the van, van old the, the van old. Try all the combinations and then together put it right.

Do this for other descriptions. Your child, of course, understands which is the correct version because she knows what sounds right. By doing this you emphasize that words, to be effective, must go in a particular order.

## Using more than one descriptive word

You can develop this game on another day into one in which you use several descriptive words. For example, you could write, 'The van'; she chooses one and you then have to write another word in a different colour: 'The yellow van' (if there are two yellow vans). Now you need to write another word: 'The old yellow van', and if there are two old yellow vans you may need to write yet another word: 'The dirty, old, yellow van'. Hopefully, you have now identified the van that you wanted! You can have fun playing detectives together: either you or your child add one word at a

time until the object that you were thinking of is identified.

To encourage your child to think in this way about the objects, see if she would like to create her own labels for her farm, garage etc. You could then use them to combine them into a story, which you can either tell, write together or she can write, depending on what suits the moment.

In a Montessori school children play the games that follow and use symbols as another guideline. The purpose of the symbols is to highlight the pattern created when we put words together in a particular way. If your child attends a Montessori school then the school will do these activities and you will just need to follow up at home using all the different objects that you have there. If she does not go to a Montessori school you may wish to make the symbols and add them to the sentences.

## Making the symbols

For this activity you will need to make three different-sized triangles, in three different colours. When cutting them out you could make them from sticky paper so that your child can actually stick them on to sentences that she has constructed.

### You will need

Small light blue triangles, medium-sized dark blue triangles and large

LEFT **You can help your child discover how adjectives can assist in describing objects by playing the Reading for Meaning game.**

RIGHT **Certain words join other words together. Choose toys or objects from around the house to provide a context. Here the differently coloured Lego bricks and the small posy of flowers remind your child that phrases – like objects – can be separated out or linked up together.**

the green leg

the red lego

the blue lego

the pink

the red rose and

eam rose and

black triangles – see the templates provided in Chapter 9.

Tell your child that you are going to make a pattern out of the triangles by asking questions. Take a phrase such as 'the large van'. Ask her to identify the word that told her what it was you were thinking of. If you need to make it clearer you could ask her, 'Did I want a car, a bus or something else?' She should be able to identify the word 'van' and put the black triangle above it. Now ask her what word told her which van you wanted. Or you could ask, 'What kind of van did I want?' Your child should point to 'old'. Put the medium-blue triangle over that word. Then you could explain that the word 'the' tells us that there was a particular van that was required and if it had been any van you would have written 'a'. The symbol you use for the word that tells you if you wanted a particular van or just any one is the small blue triangle. Continue to ask the questions and place the symbols for as many of the phrases you have written.

### Looking at the way words can be joined together

We are going to simply look at the word 'and' as other joining words such as 'but' would be rather too difficult at this stage.

#### You will need

Objects that can be joined together (see below). Two pens, paper and pink symbols that look like hyphens.

#### How to play

Take several objects that can literally be joined together, such as lego blocks, flowers and so on. Write out a label for each individual one – for instance, 'the red lego brick', 'the blue lego brick', 'the yellow lego brick'.

Ask your child to read the labels then to match them to the appropriate bricks. In a different colour write the word 'and' twice.

Place the first 'and' between the two phrases she has identified then have her read and join the two bricks together. 'The red lego brick and the blue lego brick'. Now add the second 'and', the last phrase and the third object. Have your child read and join them all together. Of course two ands is not grammatically fantastic but it serves to make the point.

Find out where the 'ands' need to go by moving around the phrase. 'The blue lego and and the red lego yellow lego'. Keep going until it makes sense again.

Ask her to put on the symbols for the words that she knows then ask her which word told her to join them all together. Show her the pink bar which you now place over the two 'ands'.

Using the phrases that you and your child have written for the garage, farm etc., join up as many different pieces as she wants to. She can make up sentences, using the joining word and stick the symbols over the top.

### Using the comma

At a later stage, around the time when you are looking at punctuation (see Chapter 8), you could create a long list of objects using the 'and' then show her how to avoid using 'and' all the time by using commas until you get to the last object. You can play around with this idea using the 'ands' with a variety of different objects, for example from your fridge, from the toy box and so on, then removing them all except the last one and putting in commas.

### Investigating the preposition

Use any objects in which you can alter the place of one set of objects easily. For example the dolls' house would be good, or simply use some pencils and a pencil case.

#### You will need

The objects as above, and some green crescent moon shapes (in the same way as you made the triangles). You'll also need pens, paper and scissors as before.

### How to play

Write a long phrase such as:

The red pencil and the blue pencil and the green pencil.

Have your child read and put the pencils in their appropriate place above the phrase. Then write 'The long pencil case'. Have her put the case over this phrase. Now, using a different colour, write the word 'in'. Place it between the two phrases, have her read it and place the pencils in the pencil case. Write the word 'beside', have your child read it and take the pencils out of the case and put them beside the case. Finally, write the word 'under' and have her read and interpret this. Continue in this way for as long as she enjoys it.

Mix up the phrases you have written to see if she can read them and tell you what makes sense. You'll both discover that sometimes you can swap the objects over and the phrase will still make sense and sometimes you can't.

The pencil case in the pencils

The pencil case next to the pencils

The pencils next to the pencil case

Use all sorts of words such as:

beside, beyond, next to, with, behind and so on.

Ask your child to put symbols over all the words she knows, then ask her which word told her where to put them. For a word that tells us 'where' we place a green moon above it. Of course there are many different kinds of preposition, but stick to the one that she can physically interpret, that of place.

Now put out the garage, house whatever in a muddle. Write, or have her write or have

already prepared, a great many cards that describe prepositions of place for her to use, and phrases that describe the objects. Ask her to gradually tidy up the place using prepositions.

## Identifying verbs and adverbs

Moving on to look at verbs, you can to do this with children by acting.

### You will need

Paper, pen and large red circles or discs (made in the same way as you made the triangles for the verbs) and orange circles for the adverbs

### How to play

Play the game first to identify verbs. Write an action on a piece of paper and have her act it out. Emphasize the fact that it is something to do, not an object . You write down a verb and act it out, then ask her to guess what the word is. You will notice that she will always choose action words to describe what it is you are doing. Let her write down an action word and act it out, and you have to guess what it is she is doing. You will quite naturally come up with a whole variety of different words that are actions. Finally you write and she acts out.

When you have done lots of them introduce the red circle, saying we use it to identify when a word tells you what to do.

To expand the game to include adverbs, play it as above but this time when your child has completed the activity add another word in a different colour. For instance, write hop and ask your child to do it. Then, depending on how she does it, write another word in a different colour to change the way she did it. For example if she hopped around quickly, then write hop slowly; if she hopped noisily then write quietly. Do as many of these as she is interested in doing, then change the word order. Sometimes it is possible to do this and sometimes it is not: it's a question of judgement on her part.

To position the symbols, ask your child to identify the word that told her what to do and place a red circle over the top; then ask her to identify the word that told her 'how' to do it and place the orange circle over the top.

The two of you can now think up lots of sentences that describe actions and how to do them. Make sure that you act them out, as this allows you to feel what the words are doing .

Becoming more aware of what words do and how they do it will help enrich your child's use of language and her ability to get more out of her reading. Acting or acting upon objects is the key experience in these activities as it begins to have a personal effect on how words are felt and interpreted. The symbols are also very important because they offer a pattern for the mind to absorb, which tells her more about the way our words work together than any explanation that a teacher could offer.

The whole process is one of exploration. Children already understand all the principles of language at a deep level; we can tell because they speak their language. What these games do is simply to explore that language on a different level and in a systemized way.

# Creative and accurate writing

Although we have used children's language throughout this book as a starting point for developing their reading and writing skills, it is important to recognize that there are significant differences between spoken and written language.

When we speak, we are able to check as we go along whether the person listening has understood what we are saying, and to go back and clarify, repeat or explain what it was that we wanted to say. When we write, we need to be much more precise in the way that we use words, and in the logic and sequencing of our thoughts. In addition, when we speak, we use body language to add to what we say: we can raise an eyebrow, point our finger or use our hands to elaborate our speech. When we write, our words need to convey information that we would normally pick up through our different senses; they need to have the power to conjure up the situation in our heads as if we were there. Writing also has the power to use time in a different way from the way that we use it in speech. When writing, it is possible to move forwards and backwards in time, to stop still for long periods of time when the thoughts of someone are being conveyed – yet the story line must be strong, the logical thread maintained. Stories also have a specific structure: in simple terms, they have a beginning, middle and end; usually, the story moves from a given set of circumstances through to a resolution.

The games you have played in the previous chapters will have helped enrich your child's vocabulary, made her aware of the way stories are written and given her a 'feel' for the way in which words can be used to convey thoughts. You can now go back and play some of these games in a way that will help your child formulate her thoughts in story form.

Remember that your child is an author. There are many perspectives that authors can take when they choose to write a story: sometimes they are autobiographical, for instance – children love to tell stories about themselves and the events that have happened to them. They particularly like to tell stories about things that amused them. And they especially like to write about things they consider mischievous: a favourite story in our house tells of the time that my children filled up the bath with cold water and tricked their father into jumping into it!

Stories like these can be relatively easy to structure since there's nearly always a denouement. In addition, your child will have lived the event and will be able to embellish the simple facts with extra details if you ask her about it.

Stories can also be told through the technique a reporter might use to retell events that have happened – a straight reporting of fact. Stories like this are often characterized by the words 'and then...'. This type of story could be written after a visit to the park or a museum, for instance.

Stories can sometimes be reworked or retold stories that she already knows. A six year-old friend of mind spent all morning writing her own version of Sleeping Beauty.

There will be times when your child would like to write her own story but can't think of the subject she wants to write about. Try not to be discouraged when she rejects your suggestions but still wants you to make more suggestions.

It can be helpful to think of a reason for writing down a story. Giving your child's writing purpose is very important. Most of us write things down for a reason and it's the same with writing a story: either we write it because we want to make more permanent something that we are thinking of, or because we want to have someone read what we have put down. Authors write with the idea that someone will read what they have written. Treating her story as interesting and important in its own right and returning to read it again can be important indicators to her that it was worth the effort. Helping your child to create a book from her story and perhaps 'publishing' it may be appropriate. Here you would need the help of a word processor or at the very least a photocopier.

Illustrations can be very useful for storywriters – they can be used to enhance the story after it has been written, or they can be used as the base around which the story can be constructed. Beware, however, of making your child think that if she is writing a story then she should also be drawing, or vice versa. Not all children like drawing and some don't feel that they are very good at it, for whatever reason. If writing and drawing are felt to go hand in hand, the fact of one may discourage the act of the other.

In helping your child to write well you will need to help her to structure her stories effectively. You will need to encourage her to use awareness of the way words function, you will need to help her to savour the words that she chooses and you will need to give her an ability to use punctuation effectively. In doing all this you will give your child the opportunity to become a powerful communicator.

## Helping with the structure of a story

Age: around 6

In Chapter 3 you looked at the Question Game that helped children to think about and expand their ideas around a topic that was familiar to them. In order to develop her ability to relate to one theme rather than many, you asked your child lots of questions and gradually built up information that was relevant and could be turned into a story.

You can now use this same game to develop your child's ability to write and structure stories.

### What you will need

Paper and pencil for yourself and your child.

### How to play

You can suggest that you and your child are going to play a game. In the game you are going to ask lots of questions and the two of you will write down the answers. Follow the same line of questioning that you did when you played this game verbally with your child.

First you need to agree on a topic or subject for your story. Sticking roughly to the subject of the original game, you could say, 'Let's write about the time you baked a chocolate cake and the cake mixer went wrong!' Make it clear you intend to write a story about this event but that you don't need to stick to the facts of what happened, as this is a story and a writer can make anything happen in a story that they would like to happen!

What could we call our story?

*The day I baked a cake*

Let's begin by thinking **who** this story is all about.

**What** can you tell me about the character?

**When** did you bake the cake?

**Where** did you bake the cake?

**Why** did you want to bake a cake?

**How** did you bake the cake?

**With whom** did you bake the cake?

**What** happened when you baked the cake?

**How** did you feel?

**How** did the other people in the story feel?

To each of these questions there will be many answers and, through discussion, you'll discover a variety of possibilities. As answers are given, record them on one of your sheets of paper with a word prompt such as Why? or How? Record as much as is relevant. Try to elicit more than one-word answers and write down more than one possibility if it comes up.

For example,

*Why bake a cake?*

Because I like eating chocolate cake; because I was hungry; it was my birthday; we had Grandma and Grandpa coming for lunch.

There are no right or wrong answers and unless your child insists, you do not have to stick to the facts of a real 'true life' story. Having gathered the raw data on the story you need to help her to understand the structure of the story.

### Planning the story

Establish whether this story is going to have pictures or not. Decide whether to write the story first or draw the pictures first.

Before you write the story with your child

ABOVE **Help your child structure the story in the Question Game by asking lots of questions to identify the beginning, middle and end – putting these different stages on differently coloured paper so it will be easy to put together the story when you've finished.**

begin by explaining that every story has three parts. The first part is the beginning, which sets the scene so that when you read the story you know:

**who** it's about

**when** it takes place

**where** it takes place

and anything else that might be important to say so that the person reading the story can understand it from the beginning.

The second part of the story is the middle; usually in the middle of a story we explain what happens to the characters that our story is about. We shall need to know:

**what** happens

**how** things happen

**why** they happen

Record answers to all these questions. Finally, our story has to have an ending. An ending can be happy or sad, funny or serious. But you need to finish the story. We shall need to know :

**how** the story ended.

Write down some ways that the story could have ended. As you have read to your child many times she will be familiar with a variety of ways in which stories can end.

Over the years I have noticed that very young children seem to be very close to the storytelling tradition and are not self-conscious about writing. Many of them seem, quite spontaneously, to begin stories with 'One day...' and end them with the equivalent of 'and they all lived happily ever after'.

### *Writing the story*
You and your child can write a story together using the outline that you wrote. Explain that when a writer writes a story she may choose what she wants to say and how much she wants to say. Writing a story does not mean including everything, rather choosing what will suit the writer best.

Write the title of the story then begin to choose how to start the story. Follow your child's advice; you could even take it in turns writing or you could act as scribe on this occasion.

Choose what you want to say, the words that you want to use in discussion with your child.

When you get to the end make sure that the story is really finished. If you like you can write END or THE END at the end. Children seem to like this as it gives them a real satisfaction at having finished something.

After this first attempt encourage your child to write stories as often as she wishes, bearing in mind the questions that need answering if a story is to be really good.

## Writing poetry
It is important not just to look at the structure of story writing and forget about the other kinds of writing that may be fun to understand. The art of poetry writing also needs to have some help. Children have always loved poems and rhymes, and as well as these being important in their own right, they have helped to underpin much of the reading and writing that your child is now doing. A child's natural love of rhythm and rhyme will lead her to spontaneously create poems from her earliest work with the Moveable Alphabet. Part of the appeal of a poem is the way that it is set out on a page: the way that each new sentence begins on a new line and in a very few words conveys a great deal.

You can also study different kinds of poems, for instance nonsense rhymes and verse, and look at the different ways in which these poems work.

Having established a framework for helping your child begin to structure her stories and poems, you will need to begin to look at the way in which punctuation can help to make a story more readable.

Recognizing the way in which simple punctuation is used will also help in the way your child understands what she is reading. You will probably find that by the age of six she is moving from reading aloud to reading silently to herself. Don't insist that she reads aloud all the time; there is a very great difference between reading aloud for your own comprehension of what you read and reading aloud to other people. Reading aloud to others is a great art and needs to be practised. Unless your child is a fluent reader, it is not a good idea to insist on her reading aloud to others unless it happens spontaneously. However, a knowledge of punctuation and how it works will help her enormously when she comes to interpret what she reads, and will help her to put more expression into her voice as a consequence of this. If you see, for example, a question mark at the end of a sentence your voice will automatically use the tone that is normal when a question is asked. On recognizing speech marks, it becomes possible to take on the character of the person who is perceived to be speaking.

From around the age of three and a half, as you read to your child you drew attention to capital letters, question marks, full stops/periods and speech marks in a natural and incidental way. As she began writing, you explained various conventions such as capital letters at the beginning of a sentence and full stops/periods at the end. When you were looking at the way that 'and' is used as a conjunction, you tackled the idea of using the comma when there was a list of items that belonged together. So in many ways you have informally begun to look at punctuation.

If you wish to highlight this aspect of writing more clearly there are games that you can play with your child.

## Punctuation games

You will need to decide which marks you are going to look at. Don't focus on them all at once. A possible way of dividing them up would be as follows:

◆ Capital letters at the beginning of sentences and full stops/periods at the end.

RIGHT **Learning about punctuation can be fun! Especially when you have to guess where to put the missing capital letters and full stops in the story.**

◆ Capital letters at the beginning of important nouns such as names of people and places.
◆ Speech marks to highlight when someone is talking, including the comma that follows.
◆ Question marks.
◆ Commas used for a list of items.

Naturally there are other marks that you may wish to introduce, such as exclamation marks and commas that are used in many more complex ways than those mentioned above. Try to keep it as simple and clear as possible: you aren't 'teaching' your child punctuation but helping her to recognize it in her own reading and apply it when she feels able to in her story and poetry writing.

### What you will need

For each different topic you will need to prepare a little story. If you aren't feeling very creative it would be alright to look into one of your children's favourite story books and copy something from there. Choose something short! Depending on which speech mark you wish your child to focus on, write everything

out normally except that when you come to, for example, a capital letter and a full stop, you will write that in a different colour. On a second sheet of paper you will write out the same story. However, whenever you come to a capital letter you will write this in lowercase, in the same colour pen as the rest of the piece. When you come to a full stop/period you will miss it out altogether but leave a little gap for it to be inserted at a later date. You will also need to write out each capital letter and full stop/period that you left out on small squares of paper in coloured pen. (Or if it would be more stimulating for her, just cut little squares of paper and she can fill in the correct punctuation on them as she goes along.) Make sure that the size is correct for the prepared story they will have to fit into.

### How to play

Take the correct version of the story and read it through with your child, using your voice to show the pause and breath that you take when you come to the full stop/period. Then look at the other version of the same story: this time read it through without pausing at the end of sentences, running one into the other, stopping whenever you actually run out of breath to take one. This makes the story a very funny one and illustrates well the function of the full stop/period. Produce the missing punctuation and ask your child to help correct the story that has left it all out. Show her that you have capital letters for the beginning of the

sentence and full stops/periods for the end. Give her the opportunity to go through the incorrect story adding in the correct punctuation. Read it through at the end to see if it sounds right.

To begin with, if your child finds this difficult she can copy the original piece of writing but if she can manage without doing this, encourage her to do so. When she has finished she can check at the end what she has done with the original.

Quite often when you have spent a little time on this activity, you will see an over-use of punctuation for a time in her stories and poems. Very often the full stop/period, in particular, turns up in abundance for a short while after this game and also the question mark becomes very popular, not least because children seem to like to draw it!

## Letter writing

You can now begin to show your child some of the conventions used when we write letters.

RIGHT **Children love to send letters, so as soon as your child is confident in her writing show her how to create a margin (using a margin maker, see page 95). Point out where the address goes and how you begin and end.**

Show her how to put her own address on the letter and the date. Explain the normal way of beginning and ending a letter. Take an envelope, divide it into four and show her that the address usually begins in the first quadrant and that it can proceed vertically from that point. Encourage her to write to other people.

## Spelling

Quite naturally and spontaneously your child has been developing her ability to spell accurately: the more she reads the better her spelling has become. You have played many games that will help her to become more fluent in her reading, and these too will have helped in spelling. Being able to spell well does not necessarily mean someone is more intelligent or more widely read than another – there are some very good writers who have terrible trouble with their spelling and some very good 'spellers' who can't write at all. Having said that, of course it's helpful if spelling is more often correct than incorrect. The more experience I have with children who are naturally good spellers, the more convinced I am that although some combinations of letters need to be learned, a good speller is one who senses the patterns in words. She is someone who is able to apply a knowledge of pattern to the abstract art of spelling. I am convinced that this ability has been developed from an early age and that it is a combination of :

◆ The ability to recognize similarity and difference in patterns.

◆ The ability to compare and contrast patterns.

◆ To have a good sense of shape.

◆ To be able to predict likely sequences.

◆ To be able to have a go without fear of failure.

All of these skills have been developed in children long before they come to even thinking about the need to spell.

In addition, the sound-letter approach which your child used in the Moveable Alphabet helped her to gain confidence in writing things down without worry or fear of having to get it right. She was able to build words, sometimes breaking them down into component parts when they were very long and building them up syllable by syllable. She also has very good sound and rhyme recognition skills and so she understands that a word that sounds like another word may very well be spelled like it too.

She can hear the difference between 'provision' and 'station' and will be able to apply the 'sion' to words like 'television' and the 'tion' to words such as 'caution'.

Without necessarily being aware of it, in playing the activities earlier in the book you will have been indirectly preparing your child to become good at spelling.

Learning lists of spelling at home will not really be very productive because a list has no real purpose. Spelling games are much more fun to play. Here are some ideas.

### Key sound envelopes 2

Take one of the envelopes you prepared for the version of this game that appeared in Chapter 7. Ask your child to write down all the ways that she remembers the sound 'ai' could be written – she can look at the cards if necessary. Write each combination at the top of a page.

Now take out all the cards with the words written on them. Call them out at random and place them face down in a pile. Your child has to write each word under its correct column. At the end she can check to see how many she got right by going through the pile of cards. Various patterns can be observed in this game: for instance, with the key sound 'oy' which she has also seen written as 'oi', a general rule can be observed – 'oy' usually comes at the end of the word and 'oi' usually comes in the middle.

Of course there are some exceptions to this rule, such as 'oyster' but it is an observation that will serve her very well.

### Singulars and plurals/masculines and feminines

Another way of studying words and how they are written is to look at words and how they change from singular to plural or from masculine to feminine.

*You will need*

For singulars and plurals, you will need to gather together a number of words as follows:

Find words where the plural is made by adding an 's' – cat cats, bird birds

Find words where the plural is made by by adding 'es' – catch catches, watch watches

Find words where the plural is made by changing the middle of the word – foot feet, tooth teeth, mouse mice

Find words where there are two parts to the word and only one changes in the plural – spoonful spoonsful, blackbird blackbirds, brother-in-law brothers in law.

For masculine and feminine, you will need to find words that have a connection of some kind such as grandmother grandfather, godmother godfather; words that are derived from one another such as prince princess, emperor empress; or words that are completely different from one another –boy girl, uncle aunt.

*How to play*

For singulars and plurals, give your child two coloured pencils. Read and match the cards. Have her write down the words in columns and always put the plural in a different colour. See if she can do it from memory.

For masculines and feminines, write the words on cards and have her mix them up and match them. If you have enough cards, do it one set at a time to begin with. When she has looked at them and can sort them, let her take two different coloured pencils and write them down.

### Collective nouns

Children also like to match up collective nouns and there are some very colourful ones about. Yet again make small cards that can be placed in two columns: flock sheep, pack wolves, pride lions, kindle kittens, crowd people etc.

*How to play*

Have your child set out the collective nouns in one column and match up the correct single animal to each one. You will need to have a little matching symbol on the back of each pair so that she can check herself.

### Words within words

Choose a long word such as elephant and ask your child how many words she can make out of it.

pan, tan, pen, hat, pant pet etc.

### Spelling snap and pelmanism

You need to make a set of cards with four words in each pack sharing the same spelling. For example, coat, goat, float, boat; crush, brush, push, rush; string, strap, straw, struggle.

*To play*

You can play snap or you can lay them out face down and find pairs.

You will find that your child is fascinated with the way words work and will enoy playing all these games. Occasionally you may find that despite your best help throughout the first six years of her life she is still struggling at the age of seven. If you believe this to be the case, talk to her teachers and see what they feel. If you are still worried then it may be as well to check further to be discover if she has dyslexia or some other form of difficulty with words.

Your child is now able to write clearly and she is

ABOVE **Discovering how words work can be very interesting. Once your child is writing, he can highlight the change from singular to plural by writing the plural in another column, in a different colour.**

confident at expressing herself in writing. Her spelling is quite good and she writes imaginative and well crafted stories. It would probably be the appropriate moment to show her how to draft and then produce a fair copy when she wants to produce writing for special occasions. You would not have dreamed of suggesting this until she was at this level. You will also show her how to look up a dictionary using her knowledge of the order of the alphabet and her ability to make good guesses!

She is now at the stage when she is reading well and writing well. She enjoys books and loves reading on her own and together with you. She likes to look up reference books as much as she loves to read fiction. She seems to have a way with words. You are justifiably proud because she did all this by simply living in an environment that was linguistically rich and had fun with language.

Congratulations all round!

' *"Help me to do it myself!"* How eloquent is this paradoxical request! The adult must help the child but help him in such a way that he may act for himself and perform his real work in the world.'

*The Secret of Childhood*, Maria Montessori

# CHAPTER NINE

# Templates and other resources

Throughout this book you will find references to various materials, equipment and information contained in this chapter, which will help you use and enjoy the games and activities I recommend. Nothing featured here is expensive to buy or very time-consuming to make, and all of them will help you create the rich environment that will lead your child to read and write with ease and pleasure.

We begin at the beginning, with a whole series of templates, which will form the building blocks for letter recognition and, ultimately, reading and writing. They can be used to create the Sandpaper Letters and Moveable Alphabet featured in Chapter 3, they can even be used as classified cards!

These templates are easy to make and will require only a short investment of your time to make. Access to a photocopier would make things even easier: you can make multiple copies for the games that require these, or make them larger or smaller, depending on the needs and preferences of your child. I recommend that you create one set of originals, then use photocopied sets for the actual games.

## To make sandpaper letters

### What you will need

To make the letters used in this book, you will need three different colours of card to mount the actual letters on: one colour for vowels, one for the consonants and one for the

digraphs. The colours traditionally used in Montessori schools are blue for vowels, pink for consonants, green for digraphs, but you can use any colour you wish.

You will also need:
a tactile material to make the letters from: sandpaper (as the name suggests) is the traditional material, but you could also use heavy-grade drawing or painting paper, velvet (which is nice to feel but tends to fray after a while). If you do use sandpaper, use the finest grade.
The templates, which you will find following these instructionson pages 142–149

### What to do

Photocopy the templates. Decide in advance how many of the digraphs you want to make and ensure that you make extra copies of the letters needed.If you make all the digraphs suggested in Chapter 4, in addition to the usual alphabet letters you will need:

3 additional letters 'a' (4 if you make the digraph 'au')
1 additional letter 'c'
5 additional letters 'e'
3 additional letters 'h'
2 additional letters 'i'
6 additional letters 'o'
1 additional letters 'q'

3 additonal letters 'r'

1 additional letter 's'

1 additional letter 't'

2 additional letters 'u' (3 if you make 'au')

1 additional letter 'y'

Cut out the black template letters. Pin them or stick them on to the back of the chosen paper or fabric. (Remember to put the letters on back to front! If you don't, all your letters will be the wrong way round when you cut them out.) Cut around the templates as carefully as possible and stick the sandpaper or other material letters on to the appropriate coloured card that you have prepared. Use the template to judge the size of card you need; the digraphs will need card that is a little wider than the single letters.

You may wish to put a little spot to indicate where to start feeling the letter and also a shaded line at the base so that your child knows which way up to hold the letter. See the diagram on page 73 for where to place the dot and the directional arrows so that she feels the letter using the right movement.

### To make the moveable aphabet

This activity is so important that you must not think that you can do without it! It's quite easy to make. Take the letter templates and reduce their size on a photocopier so that letters like 'a' and 'o' are about 5 centimetres (2 inches) high. Letters like 'y' and 'h' should be about 9 or 10 centimetres high (about 4 inches).

#### What you will need

Coloured card – use the same colour that you used for the background of the Sandpaper Letters.

Photocopy about 8–10 copies of each consonant and about 12 of each vowel. Don't forget dots for 'i' and 'j'.

Making the box to keep them in is a little more difficult as it needs to be quite large. I can recommend two possibilities:

Many supermarkets give away cardboard wine boxes to carry away bottles. These may hold 6 or 12 bottles and all have cardboard dividers. Cut the box and the dividers down until you have a tray and dividers of about 5 centimetres (2 inches) high. Stick them together to create a tray which has enough compartments for the letters.

You could also find a cardboard box which has a lid and use the lid as a tray.

Cut strips of cardboard the length and width of the box and make slots in them at about 10 centimetre (4 inch) gaps. Slot the cardboard strips into one another to make a grid, then fit this into the box lid.

## Other ways of using the templates

### Sewing

Photocopy the letters of your child's name and make holes in the letter. Thread up a large needle with beautiful coloured wool and tie a knot in the end of it. If your child is old enough to thread her own needle, provide her with a 'plait' or 'braid' of multi-coloured wool cut to an appropriate length and secured loosely at either end with some wool. Show her how to pull the wool from the middle of the braid, one strand at a time. In this way the braid stays intact and she can choose from a beautiful array of colours without having to use scissors.

### Cutting out letters

Have your child choose her favourite letters and cut them out. She can then stick them on to different coloured paper and decorate the paper.

Some children like to draw pictures, some patterns and others draw more letters! You could use them to make a little alphabet book if she is not yet writing but can cut out well. Help her create cards to send to loved ones

with their initial cut out, pasted and decorated.

## *To make puzzle words*

Chapters 6 and 8 introduced games using what we call Puzzle Words (so called because they can't be 'sounded out' and are therefore 'difficult'). Later in this chapter, I have provided templates for a possible list of words for you to use, but don't be tempted to make an exhaustive list – 10–12 for each set is all you need. Your child will learn many more just by reading.

### *What you will need*

You need to make two sets of Puzzle Word cards so you will need two kinds of coloured card. (Card is best as you will use these words on their own, with the Moveable Alphabet and as a guide for spelling.) Make each card 10–15 centimetres (4–6 inches) long and about 5 centimetres (2 inches) high. Choose one colour

ABOVE **Let your child help you make the letter templates – she'll have lots of fun sticking and glueing.**

RIGHT **Once she has made her letter templates, she and her friends can decorate them in lots of ways.**

for set one and a different one for set two. Keep the cards in a little box on your child's writing shelf so that she can always find them when she needs them. When writing the Puzzle Words on the cards do remember that you should write them in the same type of letters as the Sandpaper Letters.

## To make the classified cards

These cards can be useful for your child in two ways: they can be used to help increase vocabulary from around the age of two and also when your child is just beginning to read, at around the age of four and a half.

### What to do

You can make as many different sets of cards as you like. Try to follow your child's interests. Each card should have a clear picture of the object that you are going to teach the name of and each set should only contain pictures that belong together. For very young children (between the ages of two and four), collect pictures of objects that they will find in their environment. Group the cards according to location.

You could, for instance, collect pictures that show objects from around the house. If you do so, each set should be organized according to the rooms in your house, for example a set of objects from the bathroom, kitchen, bedroom, living room.

You could collect pictures that show objects from around the neighbourhood. For example, a set of pictures from the park, supermarket, street or garden.

When your child becomes older you can look at other 'groups' of objects that may interest them and the pictures can be organized in more and more specific ways, always following their interest. Wherever possible, link the cards with your and your child's exploration of the real world.

If you collect cards of the items you might

ABOVE **You can enlist the help of your child when you're making Classified Cards. He can cut, stick and paste the pictures with you, provided you have already prepared the coloured backing cards in advance.**

find in the park: a bench, slide, swings, climbing frame, tennis court etc, then do go to a park and look at them. If you have collected pictures of animals, try when you are out, to go looking for them or draw your child's attention to them when you see them. For example, you may have collected a set of pictures of pets – perhaps pictures of a cat, dog, rabbit, hamster, goldfish, stick insect. While you are out and about you can draw your child's attention to the variety of different cats, dogs, hamsters etc that she can see. If she is particularly fond of one particular type of animal (say a cat) you could make a further set of cards that would show the varieties of cat, such as Persian, Tabby, Russian Blue or Abyssinian.

You could also collect pictures of animals and group them according to their type. Mammals, birds, reptiles, amphibeans and fish. Or you could look at flowers and group them according to where you might find them: garden flowers, alpine flowers, woodland flowers, hothouse flowers. Always try to choose pictures that reflect your child's environment. In this way you will help them to explore their world in more detail and develop the vocabulary to extend their thinking and help them to talk about what they see. Perhaps your child will become expert at recognizing all the makes of car on the road if that is their interest!

### Where to find pictures for cards

Mail order catalogues are good for finding pictures of the home and garden.

If you have a camera you could take your own pictures. Postcards are a very good source of pictures and you can collect these at good stationery shops and in museums and galleries. A group of children I once taught were infected with my enthusiasm for Monet, and although none of them were over the age of six they could recognize many of his paintings and make judgements on the kind of subject matter he seemed to like!

### How to make the cards

If you wish to make the cards useful for increasing vocabulary and for reading, it would be best to collect two copies of each picture: one will be used to teach the name of the object and the other will be used as a self-checking mechanism, the 'control of error' when your child is reading.

Glue the pictures on to coloured card. Make the cards for the second set taller than the cards for the first set as you will need to write the names of the objects underneath them. Make a set of separate labels for the first set. You will use the first set as described in Chapter 3, teaching the names of the cards by a three-period lesson. When your child is reading (see Chapter 7), she will read the labels and match them to the cards of the first set. She may then use the second set of cards to compare pictures and words, and see if she

reads it correctly. If you aren't able to buy two sets of pictures, you should still make a set of labels and simply write the name of the object on the back of the picture. In this way, having read the word on the label she can turn the picture over to see if she has identified the item correctly. It is important to provide this self-checking mechanism as she will feel in charge of her own progress and this is very good for her self esteem.

## To make books

Throughout this book I have encouraged you and your child to make books of your own. Here are some ideas for all ages.

### Picture books

Draw pictures that tell a simple story and ask your child to organize them in order. You can then tell a story around the pictures.

Photograph a day in your child's life (or any other sequential event) and have her organize them into some kind of order and stick them on to coloured card. Tie it together with ribbon. If you do this at the corner it's easy to turn the pages over. If your child can write she may like to write a word or two under the pictures or she may dictate and you may like to write for her.

When she is more able, she can have a blank page opposite to write her own story.

### Letter books

Fold a piece of paper into three or more sections to create a zigzag or fan book. Put letters at the top of each section. These can be cut out from newspapers or from the letter templates, drawn by you or by your child. The letters could spell her name or an object. You could find pictures that begin with the sound the letter on each page makes. Or your child may want to draw objects that begin with that sound.

You could make an alphabet book with your child. As she learns more and more Sandpaper Letters, you can add them to her book and she can find pictures to stick in that start with each of the letters. Do these on loose pieces of paper that you join together so that the book can be added to. Remember that at this stage she will not know the sequence of the alphabet. When you have a book with all the letters and she knows her alphabet sequence, you can suggest she organizes the book accordingly.

## Story books

These may or may not have pictures with them. Don't make your child think that drawing has to be attached to writing. Some children love to draw others do not. Gradually as your child starts to tell you stories you can begin to write them down for her in the form of a book. She sees the words that she has dictated being written. Do not be tempted to change the words she uses or the sense of what she says at this stage. However, do make sure that you spell everything correctly. You could illustrate the story or simply keep it in a beautiful cover that you have made together. Be sure to put a title on the cover and the author's name. Read it to her whenever she wants. She will also take it and 'read' it.

Your child may draw many pictures that she will start to label, and occasionally she may put speech bubbles on them. See if they can be made into a collection.

When she is able to write quite well, your child may draw a picture that has a story and you can encourage her to write down a few sentences to describe it. She should be quite good at this if she has been using the Moveable Alphabet.

In Chapter 8 we looked at a way of helping your child structure a story and then write one. In this case the story comes first and can be illustrated if your child wishes. Write a story together to begin with and then encourage her to write her own after you have discussed the possible content and structure.

You can make this into a book by transcribing it on to a computer and binding it together – you can buy good binders from stationery shops. Some kinds you simply slide on to keep the pages together while others fix the pages together using a series of prepared holes. Try to make the book look as close to a real book as possible.

LEFT **From the moment your child can stick, he will beg to make his own books – from simple words and pictures they can become complex stories by the time he is six. You can 'bind' them in many ways: by a ribbon threaded through a punched hole or by putting into a loose-leaf binder or simple spiral. Fan books are the easiest – they don't need anything.**

# Letter templates

To make the Sandpaper Letters to their traditional size, when you photocopy these letter templates you should enlarge them until the box around the letter measures about 18cm (7in) high by 15cm (6in ) wide, an enlargement of around 230% in total

Where more than one version of a letter is given, select the one you prefer and copy that one only.

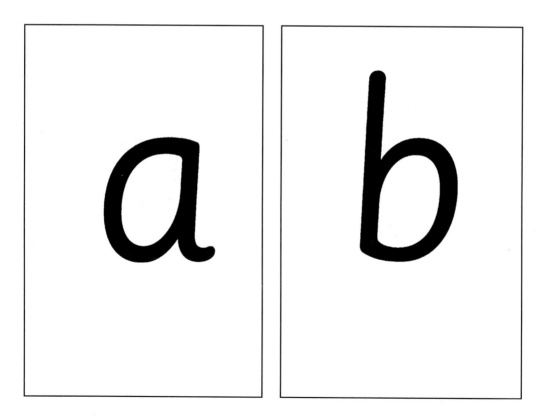

b c

d e

f

f

g

h

i      j

k      k

l m

n o

p  q

r  ૧

s

t

u

v

w

x

y

z

# Puzzle Words 1

| | | |
|---|---|---|
| to | any | hear |
| be | yours | do |
| we | they | |
| he | was | |
| by | some | |
| the | my | |
| are | I | |
| you | like | |

Puzzle Words 2

| air | lamb | station |
| fair | thumb | relation |
| hair | comb | vacation |
| chair | write | all |
| knee | wrong | call |
| knot | who | fall |
| knit | | hall |
| know | | |

# Writing on prepared paper

The samples of paper that are provided overleaf (pages154–5)will be useful for your child as a guide to helping them to place their letters correctly on paper. It is important to choose paper that roughly matches the size of her writing when she is writing on plain paper. The size in which she writes her name is a useful guide.

## Squared paper

This paper allows your child to write her letters on the base line but it doesn't limit her letters to a particular size. Encourage her to try to keep them roughly the same, using the squares as a guide.

## Four lines that are colour coded

When you photocopy these lines you will need to run over the middle lines in blue and the top and bottom in red. (You could use any colour but you will need to match it to a blackboard if you wish her to use one with coloured lines on it.)

This paper gives guidance on size for all parts of the letter. The ascenders go up to the top red line and the descenders down to the bottom red line while the rest of the letter fits between the two blue lines.

## Shaded Line

This paper will help your child to form the main body of the letter over the shaded part and leaves the height of the ascenders and descenders to her own judgement.

## Double Line with darker base

Here the paper serves much the same function as the shaded line, although the dotted line is less definite and may be left to eventually fade away leaving a single line for writing on.

If you decide to photocopy more than one kind of paper, it would be helpful to your child if they were photocopied on different coloured paper. It makes it easier for her to identify and it's also nice not to have to write on white paper all the time.

# Shapes (symbols) for exploration of the meaning of words

In Chapter 7 we explore ways in which your child can discover how different words have different functions. The following symbols can be cut out and used to create the pattern of shapes that she places over the labels that you write. You will find templates for all of these symbols in this chapter.

Keep them in little pots so that you only need to bring out the ones you need for each game.

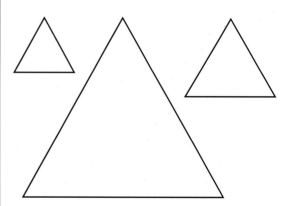

**10 small light blue triangles**
**10 medium dark blue triangles**
**10 large black triangles**
**10 pink bars (hyphen shapes)**
**10 green crescent moons.**

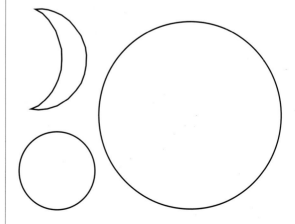

**10 small orange discs or circles**    **10 red discs or circles**

# Games that you can buy that will be both fun and helpful

There are many commercially available games that are useful and fun to play that can support your child's learning.

## Orchard Toys

### Shopping List Game

The object of the game is to fill your shopping trolley with food. This is fun to play and will help your child to recognize familiar words.

### Slug in a Jug

This is a rhyming game. Each player must find a card that rhymes with one of their cards, which they try to do by turning over a card from a selection that has been placed face down. Once your child has a pair a funny rhyme must be made up using the words on the cards.

## Living and Learning

### Unicef: I Spy Around the World

Detailed cards that need close observation provide the basis for this I spy game. Children spin a lettered dial, the first to spy something on their picture with that letter gets to cover it with a card. The first person to cover their picture with six cards is the winner.

### Animal Sound Tracks

Listen to the real sounds of animals on the tapes and match them to your lotto board which has delightful photographs of animals.

## Galt

### Picture Word Dominoes

Picture and word cards are linked together by cards with just words on them. Very helpful for word recognition.

### Letter Match

Well-illustrated cards have been separated out into three parts. One part has the picture, one the capital and lowercase version of the first letter of the object and one the name of the object. Each card is uniquely cut so that it can be correctly assembled easily.

### Stencil Set

A box containing stencils for the capital and lowercase letters. Paint and pencils are also included.

## Jolly Learning

### Jiglets

Magnetic puzzles that will either attach to your fridge or to the small magnetic board that is supplied. The letters can fit in any order so the only way to do it is to 'sound it out' correctly. The words are either phonetic or have a digraph in them: Dog, Cat, Hen, Pig and Car, Boat, Ship and Train.

### Letter Sound Games

These games are for children who can already read but need to practise. Each one has a story book and the game will use the words and scenes from the story.

Individual games include:
Donkey Matching Sounds Game
Rook Beginning Sounds Game
Rabbit Sounds Quiz game
Goat Rhyming Words Game
Toad Word-building Game
Cocky Cockerel (Rooster) Digraphs.

## Parker

### Junior Boggle

Children try to beat the timer and reproduce the word on their card using letter dice. This game can be played firstly by copying then from memory.

## Spear's Games

### Junior Scrabble

A game in which you match the letters that you have to words already written on the board. This is a useful introduction to the ordinary Scrabble game.

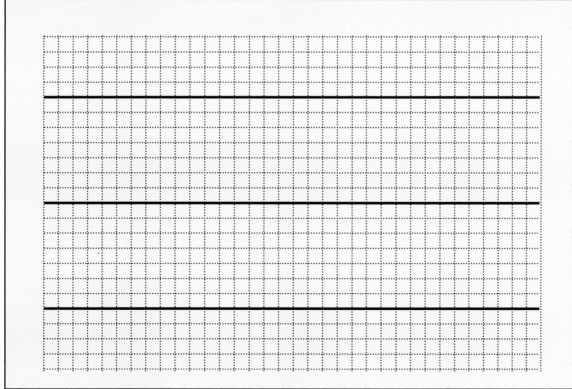

# Good books for children

I have made a small list of books that I have found to be very useful and these may help you as you search through your bookshop or library.

## Children up to 2 years

(Dorling Kindersley), Snapshot Board Books. Clear photographs and simple words.

(Cuddle Books, Random House), *What Do Toddlers Do?* Great pictures of children.

(Dorling Kindersley), *My First Look At: Home.* There are many titles in this series.

Rod Campbell (Puffin), *Dear Zoo, My Presents, Oh Dear!*

Mick Inkpen (Hodder), *Wibbly Pig, Kippers Toy Bo*

Eric Hill (Puffin), *Where's Spot?*

Shirley Hughes (Walker Books Ltd), *Bathwater's Hot, Colours, Noisy, Two Shoes New Shoes* (all in rhyme)

Jan Ormerod (Walker Books Ltd), *Dad's Back, Messy Baby*

Janet and Allan Ahlberg (Puffin), *The Baby's Catalogue, Peepo*

Shigeo Watanabe (Red Fox), *How Do I Put It On?, I'm Having a Bath with Papa!, I can build a house!*

Helen Oxenbury (Walker), *The Birthday Party, Our Dog, Eating Out*

Eric Carle (Puffin), *The Very Hungry Caterpillar*

## Children 2 – 4 years

Very often books that are interesting to this age group continue to be so until they are much older. I have included several of my favourite books in this section and find that I am still reading them to my children who are now four and six.

Shirley Hughes (Red Fox), *Dogger, Alfie's Feet;* (Corgi) *The Trouble with Jack*

John Burningham (Red Fox), *Oi, Get off Our Train*

Pat Hutchins (Puffin), *Rosie's Walk;* (Random House) *Titch*

Judith Kerr (Collins), *The Tiger Who Came to Tea, Mog the Forgetful Cat*

Michael Rosen (Walker Books), *We're Going on a Bear Hunt*

Martin Wadell (Walker Books), *Owl Babies, Can't You Sleep Little Bear?*

Babette Cole (Mammoth), *The Trouble with Mum, The Trouble with Dad*

Sarah Hayes (Walker Books), *Eat Up Gemma*

Jane Hissey (Red Fox), *Old Bear*

Janet and Allan Ahlberg (Puffin), *Each Peach Pear Plum;* (Methuen), *The Jolly Postman*

Mem Fox (Red Fox), *Hattie and the Fox;* (Omnibus Books), *Possum Magic, Wilfred Gordon Macdonald Patridge*

Jean and Gareth Anderson (Blackie & Son), *Topsy and Tim.* Many everyday situations are presented through the stories of the twins

Jill Murphy (Macmillan), *Peace At Last*

Lucy Cousins (Walker Books), *Maisy's House*, and many others in the same series

Jill Dow (Frances Lincoln Ltd), *Bridget's Secret* and other titles in the Windy Edge Farm series

Ann Herbert Scott (Clarion Books), *On Mother's Lap*

Mairi Hedderwick (Collins), *Katie Morag and the Two Grandmothers*

## Children 4 – 6 years

Some of these books will be suitable for younger children and your child will still enjoy reading those for the other age groups.

Anne Civardi (Usborne), *The Builder*

Heather Amery (Usborne), *Going Swimming*

Ezra Jack Keats (Puffin), *Whistle for Willie, The Snowy Day*

Dyan Sheldon (Red Fox), *The Whale's Song*

Susan Varley (Collins), *Badger's Parting Gifts.* Sensitive approach to death.

Roald Dahl (Puffin), *The Enormous Crocodile, Revolting Rhymes,* etc. You can start reading Roald Dahl now and keep going with all his books way beyond the age of six.

Mary Hoffman (Francis Lincoln), *Amazing Grace*

Maurice Sendak (Collins), *Where the Wild Things Are*

Brian Wildsmith (Oxford University Press), *Give a Dog a Bone, The Easter Story,* and many more.

Dick King Smith (Puffin), *Animal Stories, The Sheep Pig* (Babe), and many more.

Robert Crowther (Penguin), *The Most Amazing Night Book*

Barbara Baumgartner (Dorling Kindersley), *Crocodile, Crocodile, Fabulous Folk Tales.*

Babette Cole (Red Fox), *Mummy Laid an Egg.* A fun guide to the facts of life. Look out for more books by this author

Allan Ahlberg (Puffin), The Happy Families series. Good for shared reading

## Books about the alphabet

Lucy Micklethwait (Collins), *I Spy an Alphabet in Art*

Lucy Micklethwait (Collins), *I Spy Animals in Art*

Lucy Micklethwait (Collins), *I Spy Numbers in Art*

Michael Rosen, illustrated by Bee Willey (Macdonald Young Books), *Michael Rosen's ABC*

Graeme Base (Harry N Abrams), *Animalia*

Brian Wildsmith (Oxford University Press), *ABC*

Mitsumasa Anno (Bodley Head), *Anno's Alphabet*

(Dorling Kindersley), *The Alphabet Book*

## Rhymes and Poems

Ed. Brian Alderson (Heinemann), *Cakes and Custard*

Lynley Dodd (Puffin), *Slinky Malinky, Open the Door, Hairy Maclary's Bone,* and many more

Michael Rosen (Harper Collins/Lions), *The Hypnotiser, Don't Put Mustard in the Custard,* and many more.

Ed. Julia Eccleshare (Orchard), *First Poems*

Selected by Pie Corbett (Kingfisher), *Playtime Treasury*

Robert Louis Stevenson (Dorling Kindersley), *A Child's Garden of Verses*

Selected by Shona McKellar (Dorling Kindersley) *A Child's First Book of Lullabies.* Music included.

Selected by Michael Rosen (Kingfisher), *Poems for the Very Young*

A.A. Milne (Mammoth), *Now We Are Six. When We Were Very Young*

Selected by Michael Foreman (Walker), *Mother Goose*

Elizabeth Matterson (Puffin), *This Little Puffin*

Roald Dahl (Puffin), *Revolting Rhymes, Dirty Beasts*

Colin McNaughton (Walker), *Who's Been Sleeping In My Porridge?*

## Reference books for children

Sue Lloyd and Sara Wernham (Jolly Learning), *Finger Phonics.* A series of books with grooved letters for your child to feel that are similar to the letter templates in this book. The books also include similar digraphs

Althea (Longman), *Life Cycle of Plants*. There are others in the series

Bill Boyle (Dorling Kindersley), *My First Atlas*

Betty Root (Dorling Kindersley), *My First Dictionary*

(Oxford Univrsity Press), *My First Oxford Dictionary*

Nigel Hawkes (Puffin), *Mysteries of the Universe*. Other titles are *Mysteries of the Pyramids, Ocean Deep* and *Mysteries of the Unknown*

Stewart Ross (Puffin), *Fact of Fiction: Cowboys*. Other titles are *Pirates; Bandits and Outlaws, Spies* and *Traitors*

Gallimard Jeunesse (Moonlight Publishing) *First Discovery Series: Colours*. There are many other titles in the series.

Also look out for publishers Usborne Books and Dorling Kindersley as they both produce excellent ranges of text book.

# Books which you might like to read

### Books by Dr. Maria Montessori

Maria Montessori (Clio Press) *The Absorbent Mind*

Maria Montessori (Schocken), *The Secret of Childhood*

Maria Montessori (Clio Press), *The Discovery of the Child*

Maria Montessori (Clio Press), *What You Should Know about your Child*

Maria Montessori (Clio Press), *The Child in the Family*

### Books about the Montessori approach

Mario Montessori Jnr. (Schocken), *Education for Human Development*

Paula Polk Lillard (Schocken), *Montessori, A Modern Approach*

Paula Polk Lillard (Schocken), *Montessori Today*

Silvana Q. Montanaro (Neinhuis), *Understanding the Human Being*

E M Standing (Plume/Penguin), *Maria Montessori, her Life and Work*

Lesley Britton (Ebury Press), *Montessori Play and Learn*

### Books about literacy

The books I have listed below will be of interest if you would like to understand more about reading and writing.

Dorothy Butler (Bodley Head) *Babies Need Books*

Margaret Meek (Bodley Head), *Learning to Read*

Mem Fox (Harcourt Brace, Orlando, Florida), *Radical Reflections, Passionate Opinions on Teaching, Learning and Living*

Marilyn Jager Adams (1994 MIT Press, Cambridge Mass.), *Beginning to Read, Thinking and Learning About Print*

Marilyn Jager Adams (Heinemann), *Beginning to Read, the New Phonics in Context*, a precis of the classic text.

Peter Young and Colin Tyre (Fontana), *Teach Your Child to Read*

Angela Redfern (Reading and Language Information Centre, University of Reading), *Practical Ways to Teach Phonics*

Betty Root (Usborne), *Help Your Child to Learn to Read*

Brigid Smith (Routledge), *Through Writing to Reading, Classroom Strategies for Supporting Literacy*

### Books on handwriting

Rosemary Sassoon ( Hodder and Stoughton), *The Practical Guide to Children's Handwriting*

Rosemary Sassoon (Leopard Learning), *Handwriting, the Way to Teach It*

Rosemary Sassoon (Intellect), *The Art and Science of Handwriting*

Rosemary Sassoon ( Leopard Learning), *Handwriting, a New Perspective*

### Books about development

David Crystal (Cambridge University Press), *The Cambridge Encyclopedia of Language*

Mary D Sheridan (Routledge), *From Birth to Five Years, Children's Developmental Progress*

Jennie Lindon (National Children's Bureau), *Child Development from Birth to Eight, A Practical Focus*

Susan Greenfield editor (Cassell), *The Human Mind Explained, the Control Centre of the Living Machine*

# Selected Bibliography

### Biography

Rita Kramer (UK Montessori International Publishing. USA Addison Wesley Publishing Company.), *Maria Montessori – A Biography*

E.M. Standing..( UK Plume/Penguin. USA NAL/Dutton), *Maria Montessori: Her Life and Work*

### Books

Maria Montessori (UK Clio Press, USA Holt), *The Absorbent Mind*.

Maria Montessori (UK Schocken, USA Ballantine), *The Secret of Childhood*.

Maria Montessori (UK Clio Press, USA Ballantine), *The Discovery of the Child*.

Pablo Casals (USA Simon and Schuster), *Joys and Sorrows, Reflections*

Margaret Meek (UK Bodley Head), *Learning to Read*

Mem Fox (UK Harcourt Brace),. *Radical Reflections: Passionate Opinions on Teaching, Learning and Living*

Marilyn Jager Adams (USA MIT Press), *Beginning to Read, Thinking and Learning About Print*

Marilyn Jager Adams (UK Heinemann), *Beginning to Read, the New Phonics in Context, a precis of the classic text*

Angela Redfern (Reading and Language Information Centre, University of Reading), *Practical Ways to Teach Phonics.*

Angela Redfern (Reading and Language Information Centre, University of Reading), *Helping Your Child with Reading*

Dyan Sheldon (UK Red Fox), *The Whale's Song*

Mary D. Sheridan (UK Routledge), *From Birth to Five Years, Children's Developmental Progress*

Rosemary Sassoon (UK Leopard Learning), *Handwriting: The Way to Teach It*

Rosemary Sassoon (Hodder and Stoughton), *The Practical Guide to Childrenís Handwriting*

Betty Root ( UK Usborne), *Help Your Child to Learn to Read*

Selected by Michael Rosen (Kingfisher), *Poems for the Very Young*

# Index

Numbers in *italics* refer to illustration
page numbers

# Useful Addresses

If you would like to find out more about Montessori education or you are interested in becoming a Montessori teacher the following addresses may be useful.

**USA**
Association Montessori Internationale U.S.A.
410 Alexander Street,
Rochester,
New York 14607 U.S.A.
+ 1 716 461 5920
This organisation has information on A.M.I Courses, schools and literature.

North American Montessori Teachers Association
11424 Bellflower Road NE
Cleveland,
Ohio 44106.
+ 1 216 421 1905
This organisation has a regular journal and produces information on Montessori education, courses and schools.

Nienhuis Montessori USA
320 Pioneer Way
+ 1 800 942 8697
Mountain View,
CA 94041
This organisation sells Montessori equipment, resources and books.

**UK**
Maria Montessori Training Organisation A.M.I.
26 Lyndhurst Gardens
London NW3 5NW
England
+ 44 (0) 171 435 3646
This organisation has information on AM.I. Courses and literature on Montessori education.

Montessori Education (UK)
21 Vineyard Hill
London, SW19 7JL
+ 44 (0) 181 946 4433
This organisation has information on Montessori schools in the UK.

Montessori Trading Company
121 College Road
London, NW10 5EY
+ 44 (0) 181 960 7585
This company sells Montessori equipment, resources and literature.

**Worldwide**
General enquiries about courses held in countries other than the USA and the UK can be addressed to:
Association Montessori Internationale
Koninginneweg, 161
1075 Amsterdam
The Netherlands

Nienhuis Montessori
Industriepark 14
7021 BL Zelhem
The Netherlands
+31 314 627110
This company manufactures Montessori equipment.